BUMS NO MORE!

*The Championship Season of the
1955 Brooklyn Dodgers*

STEWART WOLPIN

BUMS NO MORE!

The Championship Season of the
1955 Brooklyn Dodgers

A HARKAVY PRESS BOOK

St. Martin's Press
New York

Design by Constance Baldwin

Library of Congress Cataloging-in-Publication Data

Wolpin, Stewart.
    Bums no more! : the championship season of the 1955 Brooklyn
Dodgers / Stewart Wolpin ; introduction by Elliot Gould.
        p.   cm.
    "A Thomas Dunne book."
    ISBN 0-312-11576-8
    1. Brooklyn Dodgers (Baseball team)—History.   2. Baseball—New
York (N.Y.)—History.   I. Title.
GV875.B7W65   1995
796.357'64'0974723—dc20   94-48467
                                                             CIP

First U.S. Edition: April 1995
10   9   8   7   6   5   4   3   2   1

Table of Contents

Acknowledgments

So many co-conspirators, so little blame...

My first thanks to Ronnie Sarig, who spent hours in the New York Public library photocopying every Dodger-related sports page from the 1955 editions of The New York Times, The New York Daily News and the Sporting News to make my research much easier, and for making like a bloodhound and uncovering the more obscure photographs in this book.

To Kevin Lynch, who shepherded this project through job changes, office-closings, cross-country moves, earthquakes, executive disappearances, and alternately having too much time and not enough time to get things done, all with a deer-caught-in-the-headlights look on his face.

To Connie Baldwin, who meticulously designed this volume while seemingly standing on her head and repeating the Kama Sutra, and who sat through my lectures of Dodger historical minutiae without once letting on how bored she was, and to Lynn Baldinger, who heroically completed the mechanicals in record-breaking time.

To my sister, Marilyn, my former lunch buddy Stuart Goldstein and my mentor, Howard Blumenthal, who all reverently read through several early versions of the manuscript and helped boost an already overly-inflated ego.

To Sandy Koufax for acknowledging my existence.

Special nods to Elliott Gould, whose unique viewpoint and enthusiasm helped inspire me, Johnny Podres who let me nervously pester him for 20 minutes, Prof. James Shenton of Columbia University for filing down the rough edges on my amateur attempt at historical dissertation, Bonnie Crosby for last-minute access to the photo archives of her late father, official Dodger photographer Barney Stein, Arlene and Daniel Mittleman of Photographic Memories for their early pictures of Brooklyn, and Lenny Shostack at Sarge's Deli on Third Avenue in Manhattan for our weekly chats about the Mets and excellent tuna salad sandwiches.

A tip-of-the-cap to Brent Shyer and Vicki Johnson of the Los Angeles

Dodgers, Leigh Tobin of the Philadelphia Phillies, John Moore, John Fahey, Peter Laskowich, my cousin Susan Post, Tom Tassone, Bob Genalo Jr., and my mom (the former Edith Keizerstein) for finding me many Brooklyn folks to interview.

My sincerest appreciation to the three dozen-plus Brooklyn Dodger fans who allowed me to barge into their lives and cross examine them about exactly what they were doing on specific days 40 years ago. Amazingly, most didn't have much trouble. I'm truly sorry not everyone made the cut.

My deepest thanks to Michael Harkavy, whose blind confidence in me to complete this project with some degree of proficiency continues to fill me with awe and humility.

And, finally, a salute to the people of Brooklyn, past and present, who keep the Dodgers and what they stood for alive.

Stewart Wolpin
New York City,
July 1994

Foreword

Brooklyn 4, New York
6801 Bay Parkway

Take the Sea Beach at 22d Avenue and get the smell of Canarsie to Coney Island at the other end of the line. Or, go the other way and cross the bridge between Pacific and Canal and end up in Manhattan.

Brooklyn 4, New York
6801 Bay Parkway

P.S. 247, Seth Low Park, the Marlboro Theater, Jack and Irv's Luncheonette. The Brooklyn Dodgers. The Bums, the Flock, my team, my time, my life. Roosevelt, Einstein and Spinoza. Branch Rickey, "luck is the residue of design." "Nice guys finish last," Leo Durocher, Leo the Lip. Dixie Walker, the People's Choice, Harold Pee Wee Reese, Spider Jorgensen. The Brooklyn Dodgers. Ebbets Field, Bedford Avenue. Our ticket to the big show. Frenchy Bordagaray, Rex Barney, Hilda Chester, an Old Goldie, Red Barber, Sports Extra, Ed Head, the Knothole Gang, Happy Felton. The underdog, the most unlikely team on earth to represent the national pastime and us and me.
Jackie Robinson, #42, the first!
Campy, Duke, Hodges, Erskine, Furillo, The Preacher, Labine, Newcombe, Cox, Podres, Amoros, Pistol Pete, Junior, Branca and Loes, the rookies Koufax and Drysdale coming up. Excitement, dreams, something to care for, something to root for, a reason to get involved. The Brooklyn Dodgers.

Brooklyn 4, New York

Where I come from.

Elliott Gould
June 9, 1994

CHAPTER I

PROLOGUE

Being a Brief History of Brooklyn and Its Baseball Team

Hot dog vendor and customers outside Ebbets Field, 1920.

In the fall of 1993, I and two friends of mine made a pilgrimage to the National Baseball Hall of Fame in Cooperstown, New York. We reveled in the town's rustic surroundings and, for three days, immersed ourselves in everything baseball, our eyes wide in child-like wonder at every bit of arcana. The Hall houses celebrations — celebrations of great feats, stadia, broadcasters, music, uniforms and equipment, baseball cards and collectibles, the minor leagues as well as amateur, semi-pro, Negro and women's leagues, and, of course, the Hall of Famers themselves. The Hall even celebrates the Hall.

But in the vast red-brick complex near the shimmering shores of Lake Glimmerglass, the guardians of the National Pastime have forgotten something or, rather, someone. They have forgotten us — the fans. Forgotten us, that is, except in one place: the single, glass-encased cubbyhole dedicated to the post-World War II Brooklyn Dodgers.

Stenciled on the small window display of varying Boys of Summer mementos such as Jackie Robinson's and Duke Snider's uniforms, a commemorative ashtray given to fans celebrating the record 10-game winning streak that opened the 1955 season, and a base signed by the entire 1955 championship team, is this legend:

THE REDOUBTABLE DODGER FANS OF FLATBUSH
There were none others like them. They had unquestioned loyalty in victory or defeat, but with defeat came their license to criticize in shouting terms — "Oh, dem Bums, dem mizz-able Bums," and it became a secondary Dodger nickname.

There was the redoubtable Dodger Sym-Phony which sere-naded with a cacophony of discord through the stands and even atop the dugout. There was loud, lovable Hilda Chester with her clanging cowbell, who loved them all — win or lose. There was even Fierce Jack Pierce, the balloon blower, who sat in his box and shot up helium inflatables. When the Dodgers left there was no consoling them and they may yet go to other games, but not with the fun they had in Ebbets Field.

This homage, however heartfelt, implies that the Brooklyn Dodgers were unique because the team had some colorful fans. But let's face it: many sports teams have developed rabid followings, replete with local characters both in the stands and on the field. With flowery poetry, tears in our eyes, and longing for a lost innocence, we fondly recall this or that athlete, this or that ancient ball yard, this or that championship season. The Brooklyn Dodgers aren't any more or less unique than many of these teams, except from a Brooklyn fan's less-than-objective point of view.

But the Brooklyn Dodgers were more than just another sports franchise with memorable players, a venerated ball park, and eccentric fans. The Brooklyn Dodgers were — and forgive the pretension — important. Or, more precisely,

A contemporary sketch of a championship match between two of Brooklyn's premier amateur clubs, the Atlantics and the Excelsiors, at the Excelsior's home field in South Brooklyn on July 19, 1860. This contest precipitated a near riot between boosters for the two clubs.

the Brooklyn Dodgers were more important to Brooklyn than any other sports team was or is to its community. "Few baseball clubs have had greater identity with, and greater impact on, their communities than the Dodgers have had on Brooklyn," The New York Times noted in a 1957 editorial. "The fate of the home team," notes historian Elliot Willensky, "represented to many the fate of Brooklyn." It is impossible to allude to one without immediately conjuring the image of the other, even today. The team and the borough were born together and died together. And in between flourished hopes and dreams.

BREUKELEN

To discover the ties that bound Brooklyn to its baseball team, it helps to review a bit of Brooklyn history.

Back in mid-seventeenth century Holland, near the city of Amsterdam, was a bustling hamlet called Breukelen. Not surprisingly, the Dutch settlers who set up their farms across the river from the New World city of New Amsterdam in 1642 christened their bustling New World hamlet Breukelen. Within four years, Breukelen, Dutch for "broken land," absorbed some earlier settlements including Midwout, which later would be anglicized into the Midwood and Flatbush sections, Boswijck, now more familiar as Bushwick,

3

and what would become Greenpoint, Red Hook, and the East River inlet, later home to the Brooklyn Navy Yard. On November 26, 1646, the peg-legged governor of New Netherlands, Peter Stuyvesant, granted this amalgamation of villages municipal recognition, four years before the New Amsterdam colony on the tip of Manhattan Island was granted similar status.

Thirty years later, the British were in charge and New Amsterdam was renamed New York City. Breukelen was anglicized to Brockland, then Brookline, then Brooklyn. In the early part of the Revolutionary War, George Washington once slept in Brooklyn Heights, but his was a fitfull slumber. In the middle of the night of August 30, 1776, he left behind some phony camp fires and, through a convenient shroud of fog, sneaked his outnumbered troops across the East River on his way to losing the battle of Long Island. Abandoned Brooklynites, however, just shrugged their shoulders. It wouldn't be the last time Brooklyn would lose at home.

Brooklyn became an independent city in 1834. By the time the first "modern" baseball game was played at Hoboken's Elysian Fields on June 19, 1846, Brooklyn was the fourth largest city in the country. Within five years, Brooklyn featured the four most powerful amateur baseball clubs in the country — the Atlantics, the Eckfords, the Excelsiors, and the Putnams. In 1858, in a best-of-three at the Fashion Race Course on Long Island, an all-star team from Brooklyn lost its first championship series to a team from New York City inaugurating an almost century-long tradition. Brooklyn teams, however, primarily the Atlantics and the Eckfords, dominated the national amateur scene, winning six mythical "world" championships between 1859 and 1870.

The Brooklyn Bridge under construction, sometime during the late 1870s.

THE BRIDGE

As baseball spread, so did Brooklyn grow as an important industrial center. Folks ferried across the East River to get to and from New York City, but the river became more and more crowded. Plus, six months out of the year, ice and cold made this trip not only difficult but dangerous. In April 1867, the state decided to build a bridge.

In 1869, the Cincinnati Red Stockings became the first professional baseball team. The Red Stockings won 84 straight games over the next season and a half before encountering the

An American Association match between the Brooklyn Grays, one of the Dodgers' early nicknames, and the St. Louis Browns, so called for the color of their socks, on Memorial Day, May 30, 1887, at Washington Park.

Atlantics. On June 14, 1870, six months after construction of the Brooklyn Bridge began, the Atlantics stopped the Red Stockings' streak with an 11-inning, 8-7 victory. But, even with the Brooklyn amateurs' victory, the future of baseball was professional.

But during the 13 years of construction on what would become a wonder of the architectural world, Brooklyn did not have a professional baseball team. Then, early in 1883, real-estate magnate and sometime gambling parlor operator Charles Byrne led a group of other gamblers and "investors" that bought a professional franchise for Brooklyn in the short-lived Interstate League. Byrne built a ball yard with wooden bleachers on Third Street between Fourth and Fifth avenues in Red Hook, near the Gowanus Canal. He called it Washington Park, an ironic commemoration of the general's retreat more than a century earlier. Two weeks before the Brooklyn Bridge opened on May 24, Byrne hired an industrious and ambitious 23-year-old clerk, bookkeeper, and scorecard-hawker named Charlie Ebbets.

Byrne's team, initially known as the Grays for their barely-colored uniforms, won the Interstate League title in its first season. The following year, the Grays' lucrative box-office appeal gained them admittance to the American Association, then considered a major league rival to the eight-year-old National League. When six Grays married prior to the 1888 season, the fans, or "kranks" as baseball aficionados were then known, took to calling the team the Bridegrooms, or just Grooms. Perhaps inspired by marital bliss, Brooklyn won its first-ever major league title in 1889, the American Association title. In the championship series, however, the Grooms lost to the National League champion New York Giants, the first of several memorable clashes between the two teams.

The following season, Byrne transferred his team to the more stable National League and, in 1891, installed the team in a new home, Eastern Park, in the East New York section of the city. The new ballpark was situated at the confluence of three horse-drawn trolley lines of the New York & Manhattan Beach Railroad, as well as several street car lines. Agile locals, hop-scotching across the tracks to avoid on-rushing commuter vehicles just to get to the park, were known as trolley dodgers or just "dodgers," and the name was unofficially adopted by the team.

In its inaugural season, the Brooklyn National League team — variously referred to as Trolley Dodgers or Dodgers or Bridegrooms or Grooms or Grays or Nationals or Brooklyns — won the league championship and faced American Association champ Louisville in what was then called the world's championship series. After the two squads split six games and tied one, the series was declared a tie. It was as close as Brooklyn would come to a baseball world's championship for 65 years.

While Brooklyn baseball teams were losing championships, the city of Brooklyn was losing its autonomy. The building of the Brooklyn Bridge had been opposed by several factions within Brooklyn and, by the end of the Gay Nineties, their rationale became painfully clear. The bridge made the political and economic interests of the independent cities of New York and Brooklyn inseparable. As a result, powerful politicians and business leaders insisted that maintaining parallel municipal bureaucracies was impractical.

On January 1, 1898, the sovereign city of Brooklyn, the fourth largest city in the United States with a population of more than one million independent souls, was officially sucked into Greater New York City, instantly creating the second largest city in the world.

And, as Brooklynites feared, provincial Brooklyn became subservient to its more cosmopolitan neighbor. Manhattan's moneyed upper crust welcomed the political and economic benefits of union, but treated its new fellow citizens like poor relations. Those classless Brooklyn bumpkins couldn't compete with cultured Manhattanites. It took a baseball team to remind everyone that there was still a distinct place called Brooklyn.

Unification coincidentally came during the greatest mass migration in human history. Twelve million tired, poor, wretched and huddled masses from every nation on earth poured through the Ellis Island immigration station in New York harbor between 1892 and 1924. And millions of these immigrants yearning to breathe free settled into the smelly slums of the Lower East Side of Manhattan and, as their circumstances improved, north to the Grand

Concourse in The Bronx, or east into Brooklyn.

By the end of the 1920s, Brooklyn's population swelled to 2.5 million, a third larger than Manhattan's, making it the most ethnically diverse community in the world. Enclaves of Italians, Germans, Irish, Poles, Jews, blacks, Puerto Ricans, Scandinavians, Russians, and Ukrainians varied not only by neighborhood but also block by block.

Brooklyn's original residents sought means to maintain their community's disparaged identity. Immigrants sought ways to assimilate. The one common currency of these people of varying cultural, ethnic, and socioeconomic background who crowded into the new borough was baseball.

EBBETS

During the last decade of the nineteenth century, the officially-nameless Brooklyn National League baseball team would be unofficially named for its managers. When future Hall of Famer John Montgomery Ward managed the club from 1891-92, they were "Ward's Wonders." When the less-than-successful Dave Foutz succeeded Ward, the club was known as "Foutz's Follies." The frequent managerial changes, however, didn't stop a club slide into the second division.

Three days after Brooklyn's absorption into Greater New York, Charles Byrne died. Former office clerk Charlie Ebbets, who already was handling most of the team's day-to-day management chores, was elected club president by the remaining partners.

Ebbets was a familiar fixture in Brooklyn. Active in local Democratic politics, he had been elected state assemblyman and city alderman. Frugal to the point of stinginess, he had an equally well-deserved reputation for honesty and loyalty. Once fully in charge of the club, he soon earned another reputation — that of an inventive and shrewd baseball team owner.

Members of the Brooklyn National League baseball club watch Mrs. Ed McKeever hoist the American flag to officially open Ebbets Field on April 13, 1913.

Ebbets wanted to bring back a winner to his oft-slighted community. He lured away the manager of NL champion Baltimore, Ned Hanlon, who brought along several Oriole cronies, including Wee Willie Keeler, John J. McGraw, and Wilbert Robinson, and moved the club back to the more conveniently located but now-rickety Washington Park. Brooklyn's NL champs of 1899 and 1900 were called Hanlon's Superbas, after a popular but unrelated contemporary vaudeville act.

In late 1902, Ebbets scraped together enough money to become part owner of the Brooklyn franchise, thereby thwarting part-owner

Hanlon's plans to move the club to Baltimore. By the end of 1907, Ebbets had borrowed enough additional funds from a local furniture manufacturer to buy a controlling interest in the team.

In 1912, to ensure the Dodgers continuation in the borough, Ebbets went into more debt to build a new baseball palace closer to downtown Brooklyn, selling a half share in the club to his contractors, the McKeever Brothers, to finance the $750,000 cost. On a four-and-a-half acre garbage-strewn shanty-town site called Pigtown, on the border of Flatbush and Crown Heights, Ebbets built his field, which opened the following year.

Ebbets Field was a magnificent steel and concrete structure. At the corner of Sullivan and Cedar streets was a curved brick facade highlighted by classical arched windows. Inside was an ornate lobby rotunda with a baseball-themed terrazzo floor. The double-tiered stands ran along the foul lines from the right field corner to a bit beyond third base, where a single-deck bleacher section extended to the left field corner, and accommodated 25,000 fans. A nine-foot-high outfield fence began in right field from the corner of Sullivan Place along Bedford Avenue, center field was at the intersection of Bedford and Montgomery Street, and left field bordered Montgomery to the corner of Cedar, later McKeever Place.

The Squire and his wife: Mr. and Mrs. Charlie Ebbets, February 1923.

Missing from the park were many of the attributes for which it would later so fondly be remembered. First, Ebbets had forgotten to put in a press box, an oversight that was corrected before the inaugural 1913 season ended. There was no grandstand in left field, and the wall was 419 feet distant. There was no flag pole or scoreboard either. Dead center was a continent away at 476-plus feet, right center was an even more impossible 500 feet. Right field, however, constricted by Bedford Avenue, was a shade over 300 feet from home plate. Despite the daunting outfield dimensions, there was precious little foul ground; combined with the stacked stands, fans were closer to the infield than the outfielders were.

After the 1913 season, Ebbets hired 50-year-old Wilbert Robinson to manage the team. According to tradition, the team then became popularly known as the Robins, and fans took to calling the jovial and rotund Robinson "Uncle Robbie." Led by such stars as first baseman Jake Daubert, outfielder Zack Wheat, and catcher Otto Miller, the Robins won the 1916 NL flag, only to fall to the Boston Red Sox in the World Series, losing a game to a 21-year-old pitcher named Babe Ruth. The Robins were back in the Series in 1920 against the Cleveland Indians. In Game Five, Indian Elmer Smith smote the first World Series grand slam. A few innings later, Tribe second baseman Bill Wambsganss killed a Robin rally with the only unassisted triple play in World Series history, inaugurating what would become familiar weirdness in Brooklyn post-season play.

Uncle Robbie reaches for the comfort of his tobacco pouch as he watches his daffy charges lose another one, this one to the Cubs, 3-2, on August 12, 1930, at Wrigley Field.

Brooklyn's eventual loss in the Series marked the end of the franchise's first baseball glory days. It also was the last time the team would have to leave New York City to play in a World Series.

Daffy Dodger ace Dazzy Vance toward the end of his career, 1935.

DAFFINESS

On April 18, 1925, the Squire of Brooklyn, Charlie Ebbets, died. All National League games were canceled on the cold and rainy day of his funeral on April 25. New club president Ed McKeever caught a chill in the inclement weather and died four days later of the flu. A year later, Uncle Robbie, now club president as well as manager, got into an argument with a New York Sun reporter. In retribution, the reporter refused to call the club the "Robins" in print anymore. He used either "Kings" — after Kings County — or the slightly derogatory "Dodgers" instead.

But by this time, the team was best known as the "Daffiness Boys," a nickname coined by muckraking columnist Westbrook Pegler, for the team's zany on-and-off-the-field behavior. This daffiness was exemplified by a single play in the seventh inning of the first game of a sleepy Sunday doubleheader against the Boston Braves at Ebbets Field on August 15, 1926.

With the score tied 1-1, Brooklyn had the bases loaded with none out when rookie outfielder Babe Herman walloped a drive to deep right-center. The Robin runner on third, Hank DeBerry, had no trouble scoring the go-ahead run once Herman's drive bounced off the fence. The runner at second was pitcher Dazzy Vance, who wasn't sure if Jimmy Welsh, the Braves' rightfielder, would catch the ball. By the time Welsh relayed the ball to the infield, Vance was just lumbering into third. Chick Fewster, the Brooklyn runner at first, sped around second toward third. On his heels, head down and positive that the ball he had hit was a triple, was the inattentive but speedy young Herman.

Coaching third was Robin catcher Mickey O'Neil, who had persuaded Otto Miller, Brooklyn's regular third base coach, to swap places for an inning. The confused O'Neil yelled "Stop!" at Fewster. Vance, who had made the turn at third, thought O'Neil was yelling at him, stopped short, and contorted himself back to the bag just as Fewster slid into it from the other side. And, following close behind was the oblivious Herman, sliding into the already crowded sack. There were now three Robins perched on third base.

The slightly stunned Braves' third baseman, Eddie Taylor, started tagging every Robin in the vicinity. Both Fewster and Herman were called out for passing Vance, completing the bizarre double play. Ironically, the Robins won the game 4-1, and swept the doubleheader. But forever more, whenever Brooklyn managed to get three men on, the Pavlovian response of the Ebbets faithful was always "Which base?"

Non-Brooklyn observers found this daffiness endearing. But Brooklynites simply shrugged their shoulders and endured the notoriety their borough received due to the antics of such players as Herman, Vance, journeyman pitcher Bobo Newsome, "Frenchy" Bordagaray (so named for his distinctive Van Dyke beard), and Van Lingle Mungo.

The Depression gradually diminished the charm of the lovable losers, however. Life was difficult enough without its baseball team making the borough a laughing stock. Affectionate bemusement was replaced by feelings of embarrassment in Brooklyn fans. Robinson was summarily dismissed after the 1931 season, replaced by the no-nonsense former Pittsburgh Pirate star, Max Carey.

In 1933, team management officially acknowledged the team's most common nickname and emblazoned "Dodgers" on both home and away uniforms for the first time. But it didn't help the club, which floundered from third to sixth place. In 1934, Carey was replaced by a character zany enough to match his charges, Casey Stengel. But the nascent "Ol' Perfessor," who once lifted his cap to allow a pigeon to fly out, could do little to improve Brooklyn's baseball lot. The uniforms went back to displaying "Brooklyn" and Giant manager Bill Terry wondered out loud if the team was still in the league.

One disgusted, leather-lunged borough representative started yelling "ya bum ya" at mis-performing players. The cry was taken up by other otherwise forgiving fans. During the 1937 season, New York World Telegram cartoonist Willard Mullin left Ebbets Field after a doubleheader loss. As he crawled into a cab, the driver inquired, "What'd dem bums do today?" Mullin's resulting Emmett Kelly-like caricature became the club's unofficial symbol and mascot.

Organist Gladys Gooding

MacPHAIL AND DUROCHER

The Dodger modern era began in October 1937, when the club traded for the fiery and less-than-daffy St. Louis Gas House Gang shortstop Leo Durocher, nicknamed "The Lip" for his argumentative nature. The following February, former Cincinnati general manager Larry MacPhail, who had introduced night baseball three years earlier, was hired as Dodger general manager and executive vice president. MacPhail initiated changes that contributed to building both the Brooklyn Dodger franchise and legend. He bought six minor league teams and hired 15 scouts to develop talent. For publicity's sake, he hired recently retired Babe Ruth to coach first. He brought in an organist, Gladys Gooding, whose rendition of "Three Blind Mice" upon the entrance of the umpires earned her instant celebrity.

MacPhail renovated Ebbets Field. In the 1920s, Ebbets had added bleachers in left field, cutting the distance to the wall to about 390 feet. A double-deck grandstand built in the early 1930s cut the distance to 353 feet, and MacPhail's alterations cut outfield distances further: 348 feet in left, 399 in dead center, 403 in the alley in right-center. A 19-foot-high concave concrete wall and an additional 19-foot-high chain-link fence created a right field wall just 297 feet away from home plate. The curving wall in right made for some interesting ricochets, and opposing players who didn't take pregame practice embarrassed themselves during the game chasing the unpredictable caroms.

MacPhail also added lights, although this renovation initially backfired.

Walter "Red" Barber

On the evening of the first night game at Ebbets Field on June 15, 1938, MacPhail's old Reds team beat the Dodgers on lefty Johnny Vander Meer's second consecutive no-hitter, the lone such achievement in baseball history.

There were two other major innovations. The first was new, white flannel uniforms trimmed in royal blue. The appellation "Dodgers" was officially revived and emblazoned across the players' chests in the now-familiar script.

The second change was the importation from Cincinnati of cracker barrel broadcaster Walter "Red" Barber. Radio broadcasts of games on WOR began in 1938, and on WOR-TV in August 1939, giving Brooklyn a borough-wide sound track. To escape the heat and humidity during the summer, residents left their hothouse apartments and homes. Folks sat and schmoozed with like-minded neighbors, watched their kids play stickball in the street or prance in the flood of open fire hydrants, and listened to Barber's country fried euphemisms echo from every window, stoop, and front yard. As one resident recalled, "You'd pass one house and hear strike one, another house for strike two, and another house for strike three."

After another last place finish in 1938, MacPhail named Durocher manager, and the two started building a winner. Their first new players were two journeyman pitchers, Hugh Casey and Whitlow Wyatt. They joined Freddie Fitzsimmons, who had come to Brooklyn from the Giants in mid-1937. First baseman Dolf Camilli came in a trade from the Phillies. American League veteran Fred "Dixie" Walker was picked up on waivers from Detroit and quickly

Manager Leo "The Lip" Durocher in discussion with three friends. From left, Dusty Boggess, George Barr, and Jocko Conlon, in Cincinnati, 1946.

11

became "da People's Cherce," in the local vernacular. The influx of new talent and the Lip's intense approach resulted in a third-place finish in 1939 and a 50 percent rise in attendance.

But MacPhail and Durocher, both stubborn and egotistical, clashed often. MacPhail would fire his manager in anger, and Durocher would ignore his boss and do as he pleased. One such firing was precipitated by the status of a rookie shortstop from Louisville, Kentucky, who was promoted to the Dodgers in 1940. The aging Durocher was both playing shortstop and managing, and felt the club would fare better with him on the bench and the youngster on the field. MacPhail threatened to fire Durocher if he played the untried rookie. Harold Reese, nicknamed "Pee Wee" for his skill at marbles, played anyway.

Although Durocher had the final word on Reese, MacPhail prevailed in keeping a young, speedy, switch-hitting outfielder in the minors one more season. Pete Reiser was elevated to the big club in 1940, and quickly won the league's batting title, despite his tendency to crash into outfield walls chasing fly balls. Other additions during MacPhail's short but memorable reign included pitcher Tex Carleton, utilityman Cookie Lavagetto, and, in June

The five original members of the Dodger Sym-Phony, from right to left): Jo Jo Delio (cymbals), Paddy Palma (bass drum), Phil Caravalle (trumpet), Brother Lou Soriano (trombone), and Jerry Martin (snare drum). Shorty Laurice, a familiar figure in a stovepipe hat, was added later by O'Malley. The band is flanked by two unidentified Dodgers and a sports writer

1940, former Durocher Gas House Gang teammate and the last NL triple crown winner, left fielder Joe "Ducky" Medwick.

The Dodgers fought hard for but eventually lost the 1940 pennant to the MacPhail-built Reds. In the off season, MacPhail attempted to fill the remaining holes in the Dodger lineup. He dealt with the Phillies again and came away with reliable right-handed pitcher Kirby Higbe, then acquired catcher Mickey Owen from the Cardinals. Early in the 1941 season, veteran second baseman Billy Herman blew in from the Cubs. Fans could sense better days a-comin'.

PENNANT AND WAR

A ragged five-man band from Brooklyn's Williamsburg section calling itself the Dodger Sym-Phony made its debut on August 24, 1941, cacophonously serenading the Ebbets faithful on nights and weekends. The trumpeter got the wild idea of blowing the familiar cavalry "Charge!" whenever the Dodgers rallied. The tuba played the funereal "dum dum de-dum dum de-dum de-dum de-dum" as opposing players stalked back to their dugout after an out, the drummer timing his bass punctuation to coincide with the player's bottom meeting bench. Opposing batters would try to foil the band by faking their sit-downs, creating a comical routine that delighted fans. The Sym-Phony, combined with the clanging of the cowbell that had been awarded to boisterous bleacher booster Hilda Chester, made Ebbets Field an endearing, rowdy playground.

But for once, the fun included the Dodgers winning. While Joe DiMaggio was hitting safely in 56 straight games and Ted Williams was batting .406 in the AL, the NL pennant race between Brooklyn and St. Louis went to the final day of the season. When the Dodgers beat Boston on September 25, they ended a 21-year pennant drought and brought unbridled joy to Brooklyn.

The Yankee dynasty, now led by Joe DiMaggio, had buried the rest of the American League and won their 12th pennant in 20 years. The Yankees, who hadn't lost a World Series since 1926, might have had the rep, but the Dodgers were actually superior statistically in 1941. But one more fluke play in a continuing series of snake-bit World Series performances would doom the Dodgers.

Poised to tie the series at two games apiece, the Dodgers led in Game Four, 4-3, at Ebbets Field, on Sunday, October 5. Facing the Yankees' Tommy Heinrich with two out in the ninth, Hugh Casey threw one of his notorious sharp curves that Heinrich, with a futile swing, missed for strike three. Catcher Owen might have been crossed up on the pitch or the ball might have simply broke more than he expected. But whatever the reason, he couldn't catch the tricky delivery. The ball bounced toward the stunned Dodger dugout and, instead of being the last out, Heinrich reached first safely. Before Casey could record the final out, four runs crossed the plate, the Yankees took a three games to one edge and the Series the following day.

Two months later, two eras ended. The first was the symbolic end of the Daffiness Boys when the final holdover, Van Lingle Mungo, was released on December 3. Four days later, the country's imperiously aloof disdain of foreign entanglements was blown to bits at Pearl Harbor.

Initially, the war did not affect the Dodgers in 1942. They lost only Cookie Lavagetto to military service, and quickly replaced him with veteran Pirate Arky Vaughan. By August, the Dodgers held a 10-game lead. But on July 19, Reiser crashed into one wall too many, this time in St. Louis, and fell with a fractured skull and a concussion. He unadvisedly returned a week later, but was never again quite the same, aggressive player. The Dodgers ended up with 104 victories, their best season ever. The Cardinals, however, led by rookie Stan Musial, put on a furious September charge, won 106 games, and took the pennant.

The Dodger roster began to take hits as all able-bodied men in America were drafted or enlisted. Larry MacPhail felt the patriotic pull himself and resigned to reenter the Army. He handed the club over to his Michigan University chum, former Cardinal architect Branch Rickey. In 1943, Brooklyn dropped to third, then to seventh in 1944. In November, Rickey, together

Wall-banging outfielder Pete Reiser successfully steals home in a 4-3 victory over the Cubs at Ebbets Field, May 17, 1942, during what would be the Dodgers' best season to date.

with two associates including an attorney named Walter O'Malley, purchased a controlling 25 percent stake in the Dodgers from the McKeever estate.

The war — or, more precisely, movies about the war — solidified Brooklyn's standing as a unique, colorful community. Every film platoon or ship contained prototypical characters — the wealthy playboy, the hick farmer, and the streetwise city boy. And the city boy was almost always from Brooklyn, and always needed to know how the Dodgers were doing before charging the enemy. The image of the tough but lovable mug from Brooklyn was given a face in many of these films by New York City native and former minor leaguer William Bendix.

For real Brooklynites, Ebbets Field became an escape. A bundle of newspapers or some scrap iron for the war effort was often enough to gain bleacher admission. The popularity of the team also elevated an advertiser to political office. Abe Stark, owner and proprietor of a clothing store at 1514 Pitkin Avenue who awarded hitters a new suit if a ball hit his billboard in right-center, was elected borough president in the early 1950s.

The war brought changes to the borough as well. City master builder Robert Moses had begun a massive bridge and highway construction campaign on Long Island. The Belt or Shore Parkway, which followed the contour of the western and southern coastline of Brooklyn, was completed in 1938. In 1947, Brooklynite William Levitt turned 1,200 acres of Long Island potato fields 10 miles east of Brooklyn into 17,000 prefabricated homes.

In the 10 years after the war, dozens of Moses-built expressways and parkways snaked through, around, and past Brooklyn like latter-day Oregon and Sante Fe Trails. Supported by low government-sponsored mortgages courtesy of the G.I. Bill, second-generation immigrant sons and daughters desiring a better life for their children sought suburban paradises in Levittown and similar developments in Nassau and Suffolk counties. The aging, abandoned housing in Brooklyn was soon filled by a hundred thousand newer immigrants and working poor, primarily black and Puerto Rican. Brooklyn was changing along with the world.

THE BOYS OF SUMMER

Branch Rickey, a soft-spoken, God-fearing man, hated the unwritten baseball code against black players, upheld for almost a quarter century by Kenesaw Mountain Landis, baseball's dictatorial commissioner. When Landis died in 1944, Rickey sent out scouts led by Clyde Sukeforth to find the best black talent available. On October 25, 1945, Rickey signed UCLA graduate Jackie Robinson to a minor league contract to play for Montreal. Reaction was vehement, both for and against, but no one was laughing at Brooklyn anymore.

Signing Robinson, and the subsequent signing of a 27-year-old Negro

Baseball commissioner A.B. "Happy" Chandler (left) doesn't appear to be amused by a lecture from Dodger architect Branch Rickey, at the annual baseball winter meeting in February 1947. The topic: probably Jackie Robinson, about to be promoted to the big club. Between the two are Dodger secretary, Walter O'Malley.

League catcher named Roy Campanella to a minor league contract, wasn't a publicity gimmick, or a cynical appeal to Brooklyn's changing demographics, or even a daring social experiment, but one piece in Rickey's grand plan to build a Dodger dynasty. The return of Reese and the still-capable Reiser from war duty, and the addition of rookie outfielder Carl Furillo, enabled the Dodgers to take a seven-game lead in July 1946. But again the Cardinals finished with a flourish and the two teams were tied at the end of the 1946 regular season. The Cards swept two games in the first-ever pennant playoff.

Two key players were added to the Dodgers for 1947. The first was a fireballing righty named Ralph Branca, who won 21 games in his rookie season. The second was the promotion of Robinson to the big club. The appearance of a black player on a major league roster sent shock waves through America and the National League. Several of his new Brooklyn teammates, led by Southerner Dixie Walker, conspired to strike rather than play on the same field with Robinson, intentions echoed by some players on the St. Louis Cardinals and the Philadelphia Phillies. Fellow Southerner Reese refused to join Walker's anti-Robinson faction, however, diffusing the intrateam turmoil, at least for the time being. Reese also quieted many opposing team tirades by a single act in Cincinnati. As Robinson endured viscious heckling from the Reds dugout, Reese walked over to his teammate and placed his arm over Robinson's shoulder. Wielding Reese's attitude like a standard, Rickey went about ridding the clubhouse of the troublemakers. Pitcher Kirby Higbe, part of Walker's clique, was sent to Pittsburgh for cash and an outfielder named Al Gionfriddo.

Durocher, who only wanted good ballplayers and a winning team, wielded an iron hand in the clubhouse and kept down dissension. But he wouldn't be around to see Robinson make his debut on April 15, 1947. Six days earlier, new commissioner Happy Chandler suspended Leo for a year for "conduct detrimental to baseball," primarily for Durocher's association with actor George Raft and, by association, to Raft's pal, the flamboyant gangster Bugsy Siegel.

Leo's antithesis, the grandfatherly Burt Shotton, silver-haired, bespectacled and sartorially splendid in the dugout in a suit and bow tie rather than a uniform, took over as the Dodgers' manager. Robinson, playing first base, led the league in steals in 1947, was second in runs scored, and batted .297. While he generally aggravated opposing teams to distraction with his base running derring-do, his coltish zeal for the game electrified his teammates. He was awarded the inaugural Rookie of the Year award and inspired the Dodgers to the pennant.

Once again, the Dodgers faced the Yankees, but stretched the Series out to a tough and tense seven games. In Game Four at Ebbets Field, Yankee pitcher Bill Bevens was tossing a walk-filled no-hitter. Pinch-hitter Lavagetto, with two out in the bottom of the ninth, broke it up with a game-winning double to right to even the Series at two games each. In Game Six in the Bronx, the throw-in from the Higbe trade, Gionfriddo, stole a potential game-winning three-run homer from DiMaggio with a spectacular one-handed catch against the bullpen fence in the sixth inning, forcing a seventh and deciding game. The Dodgers took a 2-0 lead, but the Yankees eventually prevailed, 5-2.

Several new players appeared on the Dodger roster in 1948, the fruit of MacPhail's minor league seedlings and Rickey's campaign to sign every promising player his scouts could find. Campanella was promoted to the big club, along with a muscular converted catcher, Gil Hodges. The Dodgers also added by subtracting, sending Robinson-baiter Dixie Walker to Pittsburgh for third baseman Billy Cox and pitcher Preacher Roe. A rookie named Duke Snider saw some playing time in the outfield. Right-hander Carl Erskine joined the rotation.

The mix of new players, however, didn't immediately gel, especially in the face of front office turmoil. Durocher returned to the Dodgers in 1948, but was unhappy over his treatment by the commissioner's office. On July 16, with the Dodgers two games under .500, Rickey fired his controversial manager. The same day, Leo accepted the managerial job of the hated Giants, who had just dumped Polo Grounds' "nice guy" hero Mel Ott. Shotton returned to the Brooklyn bench and, although more successful than Durocher, Brooklyn finished third, their lowest standing in the postwar era. After the season, banged-up Pete Reiser was traded to the Braves.

With Reiser gone, Gene Hermanski moved to left, Furillo shifted from center to right field, and second-year man Snider was installed in center for the 1949 campaign. Robinson moved to his natural position at second and

Hodges took over at first, with Reese at short, Cox at third, and Campanella behind the plate. Branca and Roe were joined on the pitching staff by the Dodgers' — and the National League's — third black player, flame-throwing righty pitcher Don Newcombe. For the next decade, this lineup would dominate the National League and be enshrined in the hearts of Brooklynites all over the country.

But once again, it was down to the wire with St. Louis. On the final day of the 1949 season, the Dodgers beat the Phillies to clinch the NL flag. Reese led the league in runs scored, Robinson won the batting title and stolen base crown, Roe had the best NL winning percentage, and Newcombe finished second in strikeouts, tied for the league lead in shutouts, and won the Rookie of the Year award. The team led the league in homers.

In his Dodger uniform is the leader of the Ebbets Field "Knothole Gang" and host of the Dodger pre-game show on WOR-TV, "Happy" Felton. Happy is interviewing official Dodger photographer Barney Stein, holding "The Rhubarb Patch," a book Stein worked on with Red Barber.

And, for the third time in the decade, the Dodgers' World Series opponent was the Yankees, this time managed by former Daffiness Boys chief, Casey Stengel, who was brought in by the new Yankee general manager — Larry MacPhail. The faces were familiar, and so was the result. The Yankees won in five.

The 1950 race also ended on the final day of the season, with the Dodgers needing to beat the league-leading Whiz Kids of Philadelphia to force a tie. In the 10th inning, however, light-hitting Dick Sisler slammed a three-run homer to end the Dodger season.

Changes in the off-season came in the Dodger front office. Old fashioned baseball man Rickey was losing a power struggle with jet-age investor O'Malley. On October 26, Rickey sold his 25 percent stake in the Dodgers to O'Malley and set out to rebuild the Pirates. Bullish O'Malley preferred an aggressive approach on the field as well, and so replaced the temperate Shotton with the more Durocher-like Charlie Dressen.

1951 was a year that would live in Brooklyn infamy. The Dodgers bolted out of the gate, with almost every player having a career year. On August 11, the team had built what seemed like an insurmountable 13½ game lead over the hated Giants. As in 1942 and 1946, the Dodgers played well down the stretch. But the Giants played as if they had struck a deal with the devil. The Durocher-led Giants won 16 straight, 37 of its next 44. A three-game playoff with the Giants for the NL pennant was necessary only because Robinson made a game-saving catch in the 12th inning, then slammed a homer in the 14th to give the Dodgers a 9-8 victory in Philadelphia on the final day of the season.

The Giants beat the Dodgers in the first game at Ebbets Field, 3-1, one of the Giant runs coming on a homer by outfielder Bobby Thomson off Branca. The Dodgers returned the favor by pummeling the Giants at the Polo Grounds, 10-0. The final game at the Polo Grounds was on October 3, Newcombe against Sal Maglie.

With the score tied 1-1, the Dodgers singled, walked and wild-pitched themselves to three runs in the top of the eighth to take a three-run lead. In the bottom of the ninth, two singles and a double got the Giants a run, cutting the Dodgers lead to 4-2, with two runners still on base and the potential winning run at the plate — Thomson. Newcombe, pitching on two days' rest, was obviously exhausted. Dressen called up the bullpen to see who was ready. Coach Sukeforth told him that Erskine had bounced a couple of curve balls. Dressen brought in Branca.

The Dodgers had suffered through some dirty tricks over the years — Wambsganss' triple play in 1920, Mickey Owen's passed ball in 1941, Sisler's homer to end the 1950 season. But no stroke was crueler than Thomson's on Branca's third pitch. Thomson's lazy fly to left was an easy out in any other park. But in the horseshoe-shaped Polo Grounds, the left field wall was just 279 feet from the plate. As the ball sailed over the 17-foot-high wall into the waiting arms of the Coogan's Bluff faithful, broadcaster Russ Hodges screamed insanely, "The Giants win the pennant! The Giants win the pennant! The Giants win the pennant!", an incantation that shot from radios and pierced the souls of all Brooklynites.

THE FIFTIES

Resiliency, however, was quickly becoming the hallmark of this borough. By 1950, its population had swelled to 2.73 million. The lives of these immigrants and their children were filled with struggles and disappointments that allowed them to empathize with their team. These Dodgers were like family members. They were not to be castigated, but cheered on. After all, these weren't strangers. They shopped at the same supermarkets, took their children to Coney Island, ate in the same restaurants, prayed in the same churches, drove and walked the same streets. Their Dodgers hadn't failed, it was just uncontrollable circumstances. Wait till next year.

The Dodgers responded to this support. Despite Don Newcombe's being called for military duty, the 1952 and 1953 Dodgers were perhaps the most powerful National League team ever. To replace Newcombe in the rotation, 22-year-old righty curveballer Billy Loes was brought up along with Negro League star Joe Black, who became the Dodgers' primary ace out of the bullpen. In the 1952 race, Dressen's Dodgers outpaced the Giants to once again earn the privilege of being beaten by the Yankees in the World Series in typically heartbreaking fashion.

For the first time in their now-seemingly annual battle, the Dodgers took the upper hand, winning the opener plus two of three at Yankee Stadium, and needed only one victory in two games at home. But Gil Hodges was suffering through a dreadful slump and would eventually go hitless in 21 at-bats. All over the Borough of Churches, parishioners of all creeds and colors prayed for their beloved first baseman. But Hodges didn't hit, and neither did Campanella, who went 6 for 28, or Robinson or Furillo, who each collected only four hits in 23 at-bats. With this void in the middle of the order, Dodger rallies fell short. Only gutsy pitching and Snider's four homers kept the Dodgers close. In the bottom of the seventh of Game Seven, Brooklyn trailed 4-2 but had loaded the bases with two out and Robinson up. On a full-count, he lofted a pop fly on the first base side of the mound. For some reason, Yankee pitcher Bob Kuzava froze on the mound and first baseman Joe Collins lost the ball in the early-autumn sun. With Dodgers rounding the bases and crossing the plate, Billy Martin raced in from second base and, lunging like a sprinter at the finish line, made a knee-high, game-and-Series-saving snag.

Resiliency. To help out on the mound in 1953 with Newcombe still in the service, the Dodgers promoted a 20-year-old lefty named Johnny Podres.

The nadir of Dodger baseball: Giant players celebrate Bobby Thomson's "Shot Heard 'Round the World" on October 3, 1951, as Jackie Robinson (#42) observes and pitcher Ralph Branca (right) walks away dejectedly.

Swift, switch-hitting Junior Gilliam was installed at second base. Robinson moved to left field. This lineup produced the finest season the Dodgers ever had. Furillo won the batting crown with a .344 mark, Campanella drove in a club-record 142 runs and won his second MVP award, Gilliam won for the Dodgers their third rookie award in six seasons, and the team led the league in homers for the third straight year with a then-major league record 208, topped by Snider's 42 and Campy's 41. The Dodgers won 105 games and lost just 49 and were considered by many one of the best teams of all time.

But the Yankee teams of the early Fifties were unbeatable. For an unprecedented fifth straight year, the Yankees were baseball champions of the world in 1953. Erskine had his day in the sun when he struck out a record 14 in Game Three. But the Dodgers went down in six games, dominated by the diminutive but combative Martin, who had 12 hits and drove in eight runs. This year wasn't "next year" either.

ALSTON

In three seasons, Charlie Dressen had won two pennants and narrowly missed winning a third, and felt he deserved a long-term contract. But O'Malley, more interested in the bottom line than what went on between the lines, didn't want to get locked in and, 10 days after the season, Dressen was fired. A month later, writers and fans looked at each other and asked, "Who?" when O'Malley named Walter Alston Dodger manager.

But the players knew who Alston was. In his 10 years managing in the backwaters of the Brooklyn farm system, Alston, who had accompanied Rickey to the Dodgers from the Cardinals, had managed 17 players on the Dodger roster. Alston was, at 6'2" and 195 pounds, with the build of a football tight end, the embodiment of the strong, silent type. But to the fans, he was a cipher, possessing neither the fire of Durocher or Dressen, nor the charming nonchalance of Shotton. Ultimately, he was respected, but never beloved by the Brooklyn faithful.

The team's performance under the new skipper in 1954 didn't help Alston's standing, although it was a miracle they finished second only five games behind the eventual World Series champion Giants. The Dodgers were beset by injuries; Campy broke his hand and batted just .207. The youthful Podres, who started out the season 11-3, required an appendectomy in mid-season and lost his last four decisions. Newcombe, back from military duty, was completely out of sorts, and won only nine games with a 4.55 ERA. Robinson, suffering from a variety of nagging injuries, played spottily in just 124 games. Roe won only three games.

The team's injuries were symptomatic of a larger problem plaguing the ball club: age. By the beginning of the 1955 season, Roe was almost 40,

The right field wall of Ebbets Field during a game in the 1950s, complete with Abe Stark's sign and the concave wall.

Robinson had turned 36, Reese and Cox were each 35, Furillo 34, Campanella 33, Hodges 30. To start the rebuilding process, Roe and Cox were traded to Baltimore in December 1954, but Roe decided to retire instead.

There were further defections at the intersection of McKeever and Montgomery. Head groundskeeper Matty Schwab was lured to the Polo Grounds in 1950. Red Barber, in a dispute over his salary for the World Series, left Brooklyn at the end of the 1953 season to broadcast Yankee games, calling O'Malley "the most devious man I ever met." More and more Moses-built highways leading to eastern Long Island drained more and more of the Dodger fan base. Between 1950 and 1957, according to historian Willensky, 135,000 people moved to the new prefab suburbs. Now that many fans had to drive to the games, parking at aging Ebbets Field became an obvious problem. There was talk of a new ballpark, perhaps at the corner of Flatbush and Atlantic avenues, or, horrors, out of Brooklyn altogether — by Belmont Race Track or somewhere in Queens, perhaps in Flushing Meadows.

America was on the verge of a new age. Bill Haley and the Comets had ushered in the era of rock 'n roll. On New Year's Day 1955, the United States began sending foreign aid to South Vietnam, Cambodia, and Laos. Ten days later, the Atomic Energy Commission announced the approval of experimental private atomic energy plants. On January 26, "Davy Crockett Goes to Congress" aired on the new hit TV show, "Disneyland," inducing frontier fever among the nation's youth and a fear for life and skin among the raccoon population. Two days later, the other remnant of Brooklyn autonomy, the 114-year-old newspaper, the Brooklyn Eagle, ran its final edition.

CHAPTER II

THE SEASON

Winter of Noisy Discontent

Outside Ebbets Field before a 1947 World Series game.

Quiet is a word not often used to describe Brooklyn, especially Brooklyn summers during the mid-1950s. The overhead rattling and whining of the El, horn-heavy traffic alongside crowded boulevards, the clattering of street commerce, multilingual arguments filtering out of raucous saloons, shrill yelling from apartment windows, the boastful brags of boys playing stick or stoop ball, the happy squealing of children dancing in the spray of an open hydrant, music from dozens of competing radios each set to a different station — a dissonent libretto for the boisterous ballet of daily life in a community crammed with more than two million individualists.

But 1955 began on an ominous note. From 215 Montague Street, the corporate home of the Brooklyn Dodgers, Walter O'Malley continued his diatribe detailing the inadequacies of Ebbets Field. In particular, the woeful lack of parking for his growing suburban customer base. The stout club president made it clear that a new Ebbets Field was needed. But O'Malley's concerns didn't jibe with those of the club's more baseball-oriented fans. Dodger rooters were worried more about the upcoming season.

Twenty-one year-old Larry Zeiger was one such fan who worshipped at Charlie Ebbets' aging Flatbush shrine, and who regarded his team with unabashed bravura. While growing up, he and his pals would position themselves beyond the right field wall on Bedford Avenue armed with a 30-pound "portable" Emerson radio. They'd eavesdrop on Barber and Vin Scully for the familiar "there's a long drive" call, then await the inevitable blast from Snider to clear the wall in right. To many, the only way the Dodgers could lose was through bad luck, never because the other team was better.

"Once the Dodgers got good, I always expected them to win," recalls Zeiger, now better known as Larry King, radio and TV talk show meister. "By the time '55 rolled around we were a swaggering crew. We knew we were good, that this was a good ball club. We carried that with us."

In the early 1950s, King, identifiable by his gap-toothed smile and black-rimmed glasses that he often left home, galavanted around Brooklyn with his gang, the Warriors. King was a passing Lafayette High School acquaintance of Sandy Koufax, the newly-signed Dodger bonus baby due to spend most of 1955 warming the bench. Actually knowing a player strengthened King's posse's sense of kinship for their Dodgers, but their pride was tinged with fatalism. "We also expected to lose as well. If we were ahead by three games, we'd figure out how to lose three in a row, and if we were behind three games to nothing, there was still hope. We expected to win, we expected to lose."

Faced with an injured and aging team, the Dodgers held a special spring session. Twenty-seven top prospects were invited to a pre-spring training camp beginning February 15. The last such pre-spring session in 1946 had been a moderate success, having flushed out Carl Furillo. There would be no such success in 1955, however.

In 1954, Alston ingratiated himself with his players by allowing the veteran team to more or less manage itself. But with Cox and Pafko gone, and Robinson an injury-riddled question mark, Alston already knew he'd have to maintain a season-long juggling act to keep a solid starting eight on the field in 1955. There was talk of Alston initiating major changes to shake up team complacency, such as moving Reese to second or third to save his arm and legs, replaced by Gilliam or a hot Cuban prospect, Chico Fernandez.

The single position that worried Alston most was catcher. Campy had had his broken left hand operated on twice, once during the 1954 season and again in October. The hand was healing slowly, and it wouldn't be until spring training that the Dodgers would know whether Campy had fully recovered, or if the team would have to make a deal for another backstop. Campy, however, wasn't worried. "They ain't gonna need no catcher. I'm rarin' to go," Campy asserted, swinging a 40-ounce bat to strengthen his hand. But the front office wasn't mollified. Whispers about a trade for Philadelphia catcher Smokey Burgess began circulating.

The biggest asset the Dodgers had was their relatively young pitching staff. Among the expected starters, Erskine was the oldest at 29, followed by staff ace Newcombe (28), Billy Loes (25), and fireballer Karl Spooner (23), who'd thrown two shutouts in his only two appearances for the Dodgers the previous September. Podres, at the ripe old age of 22, was the most experienced Dodger lefty. Ready to step into the rotation or out of the bullpen was 31-year-old former starter Russ Meyer, 28-year-old reliever Clem Labine, and 24-year-old rookie Ed Roebuck. Although lack of pitching was often blamed for their annual World Series losses, the Dodgers, between 1945 and 1963, led the league in strikeouts every year except, oddly, the pennant winning 1947 season. The only pitching sore spot was reliever Joe Black, who hadn't come close to regaining the form he'd shown in his spectacular rookie season in 1952.

King and other Dodger fans had valid reasons for being bullish on 1955, despite the front office worry warts. In 1954, Gilliam scored 107 runs, fifth best in the NL, and hit .282, up four points from his Rookie of the Year season. Hodges was coming off his best season, having hit .304, was second in the NL with 42 homers, and had tied Snider for the team lead with 130 RBI, his sixth-straight 100-plus RBI season. Hodges' tater total, in fact, tied Snider's '53 total for the club record; the popular first baseman popped a record 25 homers at Ebbets Field, hit at least five against each NL club, and led all active players with 10 career grand slams. Snider had his second-straight 40-plus homer season, scored a league-leading 120 runs, led the league in total bases, and compiled a career high .341 average. As a team, the Dodgers tied the World Champion Giants for most homers and led the league in slugging percentage.

This may have been an old team, but it was still powerful.

JACKIE

Jackie Robinson signing autographs at Ebbets Field, 1950.

With all these pluses and minuses, the most critical player was Robinson, at $40,000 the highest-paid, but ultimately the most priceless Dodger. It didn't matter what position Robinson played — he just had to be on the field somewhere. "Robinson became the cohesiveness on that team," notes King. "He was so good he stopped being black in Brooklyn; he was just Jackie. He was a definite team leader and inciter. He was a taunter. Robinson played aggressive and I think that brought the whole team together."

Robinson, and the club's continued commitment to integration, had made the Dodgers a national phenomenon, especially to blacks across the nation. As the 1955 season began, Robert Wedgeworth was finishing his senior year at Lincoln High School in Kansas City, which was still segregated in spite of the Brown v. Board of Education Supreme Court decision the previous year. "At that time the Brooklyn Dodgers were a special kind of national team," Wedgeworth recalls. "There were enclaves of Brooklyn Dodger fans in black communities across the nation."

Robinson was even more special in Kansas City. He had spent his lone year (1945) in the Negro Leagues with the perennial champion Kansas City Monarchs of the Negro American League. Robinson was an all-star even though he appeared in only 47 games. But that was enough to leave an indelible impression on all who saw him play, including Rickey's scouts.

Although he checked major league boxscores, Wedgeworth was too young to build a loyalty to any particular white team — until Robinson broke in. Like most youngsters, Wedgeworth emulated professional stars when he himself played baseball, specifically, in Kansas City's segregated youth leagues. "And, of course, the people we related to were people we knew. 'I'm going to do a Jackie Robinson' means 'I'm going to try to steal home,' " Wedgeworth explains.

Robinson, during his first few seasons, suffered quietly through an unrelenting and often vitriolic racial diatribe hurled both from the stands and opposing dugouts. Robinson's fire and drive, combined with his stoic transcendence of this bigotry and hatred, was an inspiration not only to his team, not only to the growing black population of Brooklyn, but also to many hardworking immigrants and children of immigrants attempting to survive similar intolerance while striving to live the American dream.

"Jackie Robinson was to white people who were struggling every day in their lives to do something better, to get somewhere, an example of what you can do under the worst, most extreme circumstances," says Stan Keizerstein, who, at 27, co-owned the Marine Park Bakery at 27-01 Avenue U. "I think white people appreciated [Robinson] even before black people had an opportunity to, until they started going to the games."

Ultimately, Robinson was more important as a player than as a symbol — at least to Dodger fans — from his very first game. "It was '47," Keizerstein reminisces. "I was 19 and we were at this party and we were supposed to be dancing and kidding around with the girls and things like that. We went into this other room and listened to the Dodger game and I think he got like three or four hits. He was the star of that game, stole a couple of bases. From that day on, Brooklyn baseball got better."

Robinson was old for a rookie at 27 in 1947. By 1955, he was just old, worn out physically and emotionally. He had hit .311 in 1954, but had been hampered by a string of nagging injuries and batted only 386 times. Alston still managed to get him into 124 games, and played him at every infield spot, mostly at third base. Jackie also made 70 appearances in left field. Even with limited playing time, he still slugged 15 homers and knocked in 59 runs. Robinson believed that with Cox gone, the third base job was his. Alston, however, would have him battle second-year-man Don Hoak in 1955.

Robinson may have been miffed at his manager, but he was realistic about his age and condition. He made it quite clear in January that he would quit if 1955 proved to be as painful as 1954. The contest for the third base job, however, stoked his ebbing competitive fires.

VERO BEACH

On March 1, spring training officially opened at Dodger Town in Vero Beach, located on the east coast of Florida, midway between Fort Lauderdale and Daytona Beach. Alston announced that no position was set and he would spend the spring experimenting with every player at every position. "They tell me Jackie Robinson is taking dead aim at the third base job," said an unsmiling Hoak. "Well, so am I."

Robinson wanted the third base job to save his legs, after having endured

Captain Reese (with bat) leads the 1955 Dodgers out for spring training under the watchful eyes of manager Alston (fourth from right) and his coaching staff at Vero Beach, Florida. The coaches (from left to right) are Jake Pitler, Billy Herman, and Joe Becker.

years of rascist-tinged, spike-high slides at second base. But the final decision, of course, was Alston's. Except that Robinson and Alston weren't exactly best buddies. The two saw in each other a competitor for control of the team's soul, and it had been no secret that Alston was ready to get along without Robinson if his physical condition did not improve. In a display of his power, Alston asserted: "I'll play Jackie where I think it'll do the team the most good."

Campy made sure that there was no competition for catcher. On that first day of camp, reporters surrounded the batting cage as Campy stepped in to hit. "Not too hard now," Alston advised. "Just meet it." Campy, as was his custom, bunted the first pitch. He then hit five solid shots. After shagging some flies, he came back and hit some more solid shots. The third time in the cage, he hit a 360-footer off the foul pole, then three longer ones that landed atop the high grassy bank that served as the left field wall at Holman Stadium. So much for the catcher's spot.

Reese was trying to pin down his old job as shortstop. One of the two pretenders for the job, Don Zimmer, said confidently that "I have a feeling I'm not going to sit on the bench anymore." Daily News columnist Dick Young asked, "When did a guy of 36 last put in a full year at shortstop, particularly on a pennant contender?" Even Reese admitted that Zimmer looked like his probable successor.

Not everyone was so anxious to get started, however. Sandy Amoros was two days late to camp, claiming he'd gotten lost on the 140-mile stretch of Route A1A north of Miami. Dodger vice president Buzzy Bavasi fined Amoros $100, not for being late, but for making up such a sorry story. "If he turned right, he'd wind up in the ocean. If he turned left, he'd get into the Everglades. How could he get lost? He must think I'm crazy." But when Campy, who'd spent years playing winter ball in Latin America, translated Bavasi's disciplinary action from Spanish into English, Sandy laughed. "He believes I said I was going to give him $100," Bavasi later explained. To add insult to financial injury, Alston didn't think Amoros was ready for full-time duty in the outfield. "He doesn't charge ground balls," reasoned Alston, but later conceded that "he doesn't hurt us with his arm. And he can go get fly balls with the best of them."

Trade talks with various teams continued, despite Campy's proven health. On March 19, the club swapped pitcher Erv Palica, who'd spent nine of his 10 pro years in the Dodger organization, for 30-year-old Oriole first baseman Frank Kellert. The deal was actually a repayment to Baltimore for Preacher Roe's retirement after his trade.

Jackie posing during spring training, 1955.

When the exhibition season started, Alston kept experimenting with different lineups. On March 27 against the White Sox, Hodges played the entire game in left field with Kellert playing first base, Fernandez at shortstop, and Zimmer at second. Robinson put in his bid for the third base job with four hits, causing a balk and stealing home. Even Alston noted that Robinson was "in better shape right now than he was at anytime last season." But Alston didn't concede much else about Robinson's eventual position, which burned Robinson. "If he's not gonna play me, let him get rid of me," Robinson challenged.

Alston wasn't angry that Robinson was grousing; he'd not only expected it but also hoped for the show of competitive fury. But he was mad that Robinson's power play was being made in the press. Alston told off Robinson, also in the press: "If Robinson had a complaint, why didn't he make it to me and not to a writer?" Robinson tried to apologize to his manager through the tabloids, but added that "I told him I can't talk to him. I don't know why, I just can't."

A couple of days later, the two combatants publicly buried the hatchet, acting as if an unkind word had never passed between them. In the New York Times, columnist Arthur Daly mused that the players had never accepted Alston as they had Dressen, Durocher, or even Uncle Robbie, and that the "teapot tempest" was Alston's attempt to solidify his authority and win the respect of his players.

The team arrived in Brooklyn to prepare for their final preseason games, a home-and-home series with the Yankees. On April 9, Hodges clubbed two homers and drove in six runs, his first RBI of spring, and Furillo crashed two dingers to beat the Yanks 14-5 at Ebbets Field. The following day in the Bronx, the Yanks spanked the Brooks 7-3, their fourth victory in six exhibition games with the Dodgers.

The Dodgers finished the spring 10-14-1. Their spring record may have been mediocre, but Alston's shrewd manipulation of his players had succeeded. They were razor sharp and determined to make up not only for 1954 but also for the last 40 years.

THE STREAK

Dodger broadcaster Vin Scully, who worked with, then succeeded, Red Barber.

As usual, all the winter sports seasons had wrapped up by the time the baseball season started. The San Francisco Dons, led by center Bill Russell, won the first of its two consecutive NCAA college basketball championships. The Syracuse Nationals won the NBA championship by beating the Fort Wayne Pistons, concluding the first season with the 24-second clock in use. The Detroit Red Wings upset the dynastic Montreal Canadiens to win hockey's Stanley Cup. Cary Middlecoff beat Ben Hogan to win the Masters golf tournament.

Tuesday, April 12, was cold, rainy, and windy, presaging a cold, rainy, windy spring in Brooklyn. Opening day at Ebbets Field against the Pirates had to be postponed. Rather than pushing the home opener back an entire week, the two teams tangled the following day despite 40-degree temperatures and a steady drizzle. And after all the spring intrigue, there were no surprises in Alston's belated opening day lineup: Gilliam 2B, Reese SS, Snider CF, Hodges 1B, Amoros LF, Robinson 3B, Furillo RF, Campy C. Erskine drew the opening day pitching honors.

New York governor Averell Harriman had been scheduled to throw out the first ball, but couldn't wait another day. His replacement, Brooklyn borough president John Cashmore, yelled to Robinson, "Catch this!" He then proceeded to bean the Marine color guard standing at attention 15 feet away. Erskine had slightly better control. Before some 7,000 chilled fans, the veteran righty tossed a seven-hitter, Gilliam hit a solo homer, and Furillo added a three-run blast in a 6-1 triumph. It was the first opening day victory for "Oisk" in five tries.

Robinson immediately demonstrated to Alston why he belonged in the lineup. He was the runner on second when the Brooks had the bases loaded with the score tied in the sixth. Campy hit a sure inning-ending double-play ball toward short, but Robinson let the ball hit him. The ball, of course, was declared dead, Robinson was out, and no runners advanced — but the bases remained loaded and the inning continued. That the Dodgers didn't take advantage of Robinson's heads-up play was academic. It was the sort of spark that Robinson could provide. He would be the spring of inspiration that the Dodgers would draw from for the next month. But first, an early two-game set at the Polo Grounds, starting with the Giants' home opener.

The Cold War had begun, but the relationship between the Soviets and the Americans was positively lovey-dovey compared to the visceral hatred that existed between the Giants and Dodgers, both players and fans. "Giant fans were probably the lowest type of animal life that existed," stated Bob Genalo Sr. In 1955, Genalo was a 27-year-old accountant for Texaco, a father of a year-old son, a new home owner, a loyal Dodger fan from Flatbush, and a typical Giant hater. "The Giants were a waste, you know, and their fans were worse."

The feud was so intense that few fans dared travel to see games in the other's home yard. "I wouldn't go to the Polo Grounds because the Giants were there," Genalo said. "Because if you go to the Polo Grounds, you're only going to wind up in a fight."

This level of intensity was somewhat new to 11-year-old Bill Borst. The future sportswriter was one of the few Dodger fans among the 29,000-plus who crowded the Polo Grounds on Opening Day to watch New York City mayor Robert Wagner toss out the first ball, Al Dark hoist the Giants' 1954 NL pennant, and Whitey Lockman raise the world's championship banner. Borst lived in Queens, but his grandparents resided in Brooklyn and his family traversed the Belt Parkway for regular visits every other Sunday. On one such drive on October 5, 1952, Borst heard the radio description of the dramatic Dodger win in Game Five of the World Series and instantly became a Dodger rooter. "The whole thing was very much like the religious experience of 'sudden conversion,' " Borst recalled in his book, *A Fan's Memoir: The Brooklyn Dodgers 1953-1957*. "I remember it with the same sort of emotional pleasure that a young boy remembers his first kiss."

Borst's first live Dodger game was at the Polo Grounds on May 29, 1954, where he saw Reese homer to give Erskine a 3-2 victory over Sal Maglie. Once again he would watch Maglie pitch for the Giants, this time against Newcombe. But "neither pitcher was especially impressive," Borst would later write. "Home runs flew into the cheap seats like birds escaping a cage." The Dodgers won 10-8 with Furillo and Campy each smacking three-run HRs. Since he was less than effective on the mound, Newk had to contribute two homers of his own. Snider's leaping backhanded catch of a Monte Irvin drive into left-center in the bottom of the ninth preserved the victory.

The catch prompted Snider to swagger about his status as New York's premier center fielder. Earlier in the spring, Snider reasoned he had to be better — he made $10,000 a year more than Giants' rising center field star, Willie Mays, whose spectacular over-the-shoulder catch in the '54 World Series established him as an instant legend. And while castigating reporters for making meaningless comparisons, Snider noted he could make any catch Mays could. Newcombe joined in Snider's chorus after the game. "To hell with Mays. Our boy is the bestest."

Furillo smacked two more homers, Snider backed up his talk with a mammoth 460-foot three-run blast into the right field stands, all supporting Loes' complete game six-hitter to beat the Giants 6-3 on Friday before the Dodgers moved on to Pittsburgh. On Saturday, Pirate hurler Bob Purkey had a perfect game into the seventh. Gilliam's lead-off single broke the no-hit bid, Snider's RBI single snapped the shutout, and the Dodger five-run eighth won the game as the Dodgers took their fourth straight, 6-0. Brooklyn won their fifth and sixth straight in a Forbes Field doubleheader sweep on Sunday, 10-3, 3-2. But the Dodgers also suffered a couple of injuries. In the sixth inning of the nightcap, Reese pulled a groin muscle. And bonus baby Koufax tripped and sprained his right ankle. Sub George Shuba couldn't help ribbing the nouveau riche rookie. "I told you not to carry your wallet in your uniform," Shuba jibed. "The weight throws you off balance."

Next came four games against the Phillies, Monday and Tuesday at Connie Mack Stadium, Wednesday and Thursday back in Brooklyn. Snider continued to destroy National League pitching, knocking a three-run homer to back up Erskine in the 5-2 victory. Zimmer celebrated his short stint as the Dodger starting shortstop with his first major league dinger, and Furillo and Campy also homered as the Dodgers held on, 7-6, their eighth straight victory.

The major league record for consecutive victories at the start of a season was 12, set by the 1884 New York National League team, not yet known as the Giants. The modern record of nine straight victories was held by three teams: the 1918 Giants, the 1940 Dodgers, and the 1944 Browns.

Only 9,942 attended the Dodgers' Ebbets Field homecoming on April 20 to see them tie their own record with a 3-2 victory over the Phillies. The record fell on Friday afternoon, but only 3,874 bothered to show up to watch the Flock rout Phillie pitcher and Dodger-killer Robin Roberts, 14-4. Duke smacked a three-run dinger and Amoros added a two-run shot, part of five straight hits in a seven-run fourth inning. In the home clubhouse, a blackboard message read: "The Bums dood it, 10 straight."

Late in the rout, PA announcer Tex Rickard announced that O'Malley,

"We dood it": Alston poses with his stars on April 21 after the Dodgers set a major league record with their 10th straight victory to start the season. From left to right: Robinson, winning pitcher Joe Black, Snider, Zimmer, Hodges, and Alston.

with ironic generosity, would award all fans who sent the club their ticket stubs an unnamed "memento" of the record-breaking win. "You know what I thought?" asked Snider rhetorically. "I took one look at the empty stands and said to myself: 'Now they're going to announce the move of the franchise to Los Angeles.' "

Reese echoed the sentiment. "What's happened to the crowds?" the captain pondered. "You'd think 10 in a row would get them out. I can remember when we'd come back north and play in snow, and there'd be 20 or 25 thousand people to see us. The weather wasn't good, but it wasn't that bad today."

The ticket office announced that there were still "plenty" of seats available for all three games of the weekend series against the Giants; in fact, there were 27,000 available for Saturday's game, 23,000 for Sunday's. The Daily News pointed out that "in past seasons, night games with the Giants would have long been sold out, box and reserve seats, even if the Brooks stood 0-10."

The commemorative ashtray O'Malley sent to the fans who attended the record-breaking victory April 21.

SECOND STREAK

It would have been sweet to beat the Giants and break their 1884 record. And despite the dire scribblings about falling attendance, more than 27,000 faithful braved Friday's early-morning rain and fog — just in time to see Podres lose the first Dodger game of the season. The Giants scored all five of their runs in the eighth to win, 5-4, in a rollicking contest that saw the usually reserved Alston get tossed for arguing a call.

The setback, however, was temporary, as was the box office drought. A capacity throng of 32,482 showed up on Saturday afternoon to watch a 3-1 victory over Maglie and some bench-clearing fireworks, courtesy of Robinson. Maglie, living up to his nickname of "The Barber," had thrown close to several Brooklyn batters. In the fourth, he plunked Campy, enraging the on-deck hitter Robinson, who earlier had had to duck out of the way of a Maglie purpose pitch. Jackie faked a bunt, indicating to Maglie that he was laying one down the first base line. The idea was that when Maglie raced over to cover first, Robinson would have the opportunity to run him down. Maglie smiled in recognition of his impending doom. Sure enough, Jackie laid one down perfectly. Except Maglie wanted no part of the rampaging Robinson and stood stock-still on the mound. First baseman Lockman fielded the ball and tossed it to Davey Williams, the second baseman who covered first.

The unsuspecting Williams never had a chance. The 205-pound Robinson, a former All-American football star, plowed into the 160-pound infielder's mid-section, sending him head over heels. The benches cleared.

When Giant captain and Williams' roommate Al Dark returned to the dugout after the inning ended, he exhorted his teammates. Someone, anyone, had to get to Robinson, now glaring defiantly into the Giant dugout from his spot at third base. Coincidentally, Dark led off. He smacked a sure double into the left field corner that Amoros was about to toss casually back to the infield — except that Dark didn't stop at second. With head down, he turned and headed toward third and Robinson, who was just receiving Amoros' hurried throw.

Dark, also a former football All-American, practically tackled Robinson. Glove, hats, ball — and Robinson — went flying. When action resumed, Dark, standing on third, and Robinson, 15 feet away at his position, spit invectives at each other. Finally, third base umpire Babe Pinelli had to call time. Both players were so busy cursing each other that neither had noticed Erskine pitching to Mays.

In a slim measure of revenge before the chilly Sunday afternoon rubber match, Leo refused to give his lineup to the PA announcer. The Dodgers protested, but there was no rule about giving the stadium announcer the line-up, forcing Rickard to wing it. Newcombe started but wasn't around when the Giants scored six in the 10th then survived a five-run Dodger rally in the bottom of the inning to win a wild 11-10 contest. Both Robinson and Davey Williams took the day off to heal. Dark, however, hit a two-run homer in the ninth to force the extra inning.

The violent weekend proved to be an abberation in the Dodgers 1955 start. The team reeled off another 11 straight victories. After a cancellation due to cold weather, the Brooks beat the Reds, took two from the Cubs, two from the Braves, and two from the Cardinals to wrap up their first homestand. In Philadelphia, the Dodgers swept a three-game weekend series, then took the first game in a three-game set from the Cubs. Their 11th straight victory was a 1-0, one-hit gem by Newcombe, who faced the mininum 27 hitters in less than two hours, the lone run coming on Snider's 200th career homer. "It was the best game I ever pitched," Newcombe told reporters.

The Dodgers were now 24-2, the best start ever in baseball history, topping the 24-3 record start by the 1907 Giants. They had beaten every team in the league and were already 9½ games in front less than a month into the season. Snider's nine homers and 30 RBI and Erskine's 1.44 ERA were top marks in the league. Hot-hitting Campy, who started off the season batting eighth — and grumbling about it — gradually had been moved up to the cleanup spot. No opposing pitcher had managed to complete a game against them.

The second winning string was broken on May 11 when the Cubs beat the Brooks 10-8, thanks in part to a first inning grand slam by Ernie Banks. Ironically, the Dodgers clubbed 14 hits, their highest hit total of the season thus far.

The hitting may have been healthy, but the mound was becoming a disaster area. Before the 11-game string, the sore-armed Spooner returned to the minors, his arm injury aggravated by the cold, damp weather in Brooklyn. The weather also affected Newcombe, who was suffering from his annual sore shoulder. Then Loes developed a blister on a finger on his pitching hand. Rookie left-hander Tom Lasorda needed five stitches to close a spike gash. And

Koufax, still recovering from his sprained right ankle, tripped in Chicago and sprained his other ankle.

Newcombe was ready to return in early May, but Alston wanted to hold him back just to be safe. On May 5, Newk was asked to pitch batting practice, but refused, saying he wanted to pitch in games. Alston immediately suspended his ace without pay, which would cost Newcombe $104.79 a day based on his yearly $17,000 salary.

Robinson, already an expert at tangling with Alston, predicted that Newk would be back the next day. Sure enough, after mulling over the financial ramifications of his insubordination, Newk reported that he'd rejoin the club immediately. "I'm no millionaire," Newcombe reasoned. "I can't afford to retire. Maybe the man [Alston] knows me better than I know myself." In a conciliatory gesture, Alston started Newk the next day and Newk celebrated by tossing 12 innings to gain the victory in Philadelphia. After the game, Alston was the first to congratulate his wayward pitcher.

But attendance at Ebbets Field had reverted to its sorry state. Less than 2,500 were present for one game against the Cubs, prompting a local TV news commentator to remark that poor attendance would drive the franchise to another town.

COOLING OFF

In the real world that spring, Dr. Jonas Salk announced his antipolio vaccine. The Allied powers ended their occupation of West Germany, which then formally joined NATO. Ten days later, the Soviet Union and its Eastern European allies formed the Warsaw Pact. A patent for a nuclear reactor was issued to Enrico Fermi, the discoverer of uranium fission, and Leo Szilard. On May 31, racial seg-

Alston explains to reporters that he's in charge after suspending an insubordinate Newcombe on May 5. "I told him, 'I'm not going to argue with you anymore. This is the second time you've disobeyed. The only thing I can tell you is to take off your uniform and go on home.'"

regation in public schools was banned by the U.S. Supreme Court. In another milestone, the Presbyterian church approved the ordination of women ministers.

On a lighter note, Marlon Brando won the Best Actor Oscar for "On the Waterfront". Tennessee Williams won a Pulitzer for his play "Cat on a Hot Tin Roof". Ray Walston and Gwen Verdon opened on Broadway in "Damn Yankees", the tale of a rabid Washington Senators' fan who signs a pact with the devil to help his team beat the Yankees for the AL pennant.

In the real Bronx, a second-year premed school student, Mike Sharff, was studying for his finals at the University Heights campus of New York University's College of Arts and Sciences, 20 blocks north of Yankee Stadium. But Sharff was a native Brooklynite, born and bred in Flatbush.

Sharff's parents followed the Dodgers on TV, but not with the same intensity as his immigrant grandmother. "She was from Russia and she spoke only Russian or Yiddish, but she knew every Dodger," Sharff recalls. "She used to go to the games until she couldn't go any longer and then wouldn't stop watching them on television. She loved them like they were part of her own family. She used to get angry at Gil Hodges because he would frequently strike out with men on base. He was what she called 'a grossa fidena,' which in Yiddish means something like the big-shot who can't do anything." His grandmother was 89 when she died of a heart attack while watching Snider at bat. "It's very hard to capture in words what a close feeling there was," says Sharff, "but it was that kind of a hold that the Dodgers had on people."

From the age of nine, Sharff practically lived in the left field bleachers at Ebbets Field, a half hour's walk from his house. He also occasionally spotted many of the players, like Hodges and Cox, who lived in his neighborhood. "There were about eight of them who actually lived within walking distance and actually shopped in the same stores that we did. They even got a kick out of people going up and saying hello and wishing them luck and that sort of thing."

When it came time for college in the fall of 1953, Sharff could have stayed close to home and attended Brooklyn College, "but I felt that it was a little crazy to feel as strongly as I did because the Dodgers were never going to really pull it off," Sharff says. "And when they didn't do it in '54, I remember feeling that Alston just didn't have the drive or the personality to ever get them to that point. Hope, yes, because they still had enough and they were still family. I mean, you wanted them to get there. But if they hadn't done it with some of the teams that they had when they were younger, it wasn't at all likely that they were going to do it then."

Busy with fraternity life, studies, and coeds, Sharff allowed the Dodgers to slip as a priority — until the 24-2 start. "That was about the time of year that we began to feel that maybe they had a shot at winning it," he says. So Sharff managed to get tickets for a Sunday afternoon game on May 22 against the Phillies. "I had no business going because I was in the middle of finals, but I decided that the game was more important."

On Sunday May 22, pre-med student Mike Sharff and a couple of his Flatbush buddies watched Snider rob the Phillies' Willie Jones of an extra base hit in the fourth inning of an 8-3 Dodger victory.

Sharff and two friends scalped tickets and sat right behind home plate. The Phils out-hit the Brooks, 8 to 7, but the Brooks out-homered them 3 to 1 en route to an 8-3 victory.

But by mid-May, baseball reality finally caught up with the Dodgers. They would lose three, win three, lose two, win two, just treading water. After ending a western swing with three straight losses, 2,000 faithful and the Dodger Sym-Phony greeted them at LaGuardia Airport. The reception puzzled some of the Dodgers because they had been losing and attendence at Ebbets Field hadn't really picked up. It turned out that most of the fans were Catholic kids, off for what the Daily News described as a "holy day."

Alston announced that Robinson would be his regular third baseman, despite a 1 for 15 slump and a .230 batting average. "I wish one of them would hit," Alston complained about Robinson, Hoak, and Zimmer. "I don't care which one. But opposing pitchers have more respect for Robinson. Even if he's not hitting, they at least know he can hit, and that will put pressure on them."

THIRD STREAK

On May 28, the Brooks beat the Giants 5-3 in the next-to-last game of an eastern road trip. The game featured the first nationally televised triple play, which provided a measure of revenge for battered Giant second baseman Williams. In the fourth inning with Furillo on first and Hodges on second, Robinson hit a short bloop into right field that looked like a sure hit, prompting the runners to take off. Williams made a dazzling over-the-shoulder grab, then tossed to Dark covering second, who then relayed the ball to Lockman at first before Furillo could scramble back.

Winning despite the triple play got the Flock hot again. They won 16 of their next 19, sewing up the pennant by mid-June. In the second game of a doubleheader sweep over the Pirates on May 30, Newcombe won his eighth straight without a loss and, for the second time that season, crashed two homers in the same game. To prolong his hitting streak, the superstitious Newcombe adopted the ritual of calling for the rosin bag after each pitch while at bat.

Attendance continued to suffer. Less than 8,000 showed up on Tuesday night, May 31, to see popular heartthrob Eddie Fisher receive a plaque from Reese and a scroll from Erskine, signed by the entire team, in recognition of Fisher's work with the "youth of America." O'Malley ominously reported on "a very important election being held in Los Angeles today. It's on a bond issue for the purpose of spending $4.5 million on a ballpark to seat 63,000."

With attendence on low, Brooklyn batting power was turned up to high,

Snider always insisted he was every bit as good with the glove as Willie Mays, here sliding into Campy to complete an inside-the-park homer in the seventh inning of an eventual 8-5 Dodger victory over the Giants at the Polo Grounds, May 29.

especially Snider's. On June 1, the team set a new record with six homers in a game, three by Snider. His second drive soared 100 feet higher than the top of the right field foul pole and landed on the roof of the Dodger Gas station across Bedford Avenue. He almost collected a record-tying fourth circuit blast in the eighth, but his drive hit the screen 4 feet below the homer line.

The next day, before 5,300 paying customers and 10,000 "guests of management" including commissioner Ford Frick, the Flock scored 10 in the eighth inning — two on another Snider clout — to break open a close game. The following day, Snider drove in five more runs, three on another homer, in a 12-5 beating of St. Louis. On June 5, Snider went hitless, but Newk won his ninth without a loss before a Ladies Day crowd of 23,000. Newk also thought he'd hit his fifth homer of the season and circled the bases accordingly, but the umps ruled that the ball went through the screen, not over it, forcing the disgruntled pitcher back to second base with a grounds-rule double. A later examination revealed no such hole, meaning the hit had been a home run. Campy also homered, his sixth round-tripper in seven games, and now had 51 RBI, three shy of his entire 1954 output.

Each time Snider or Campy or any other Dodger homered, the cheer from the Ebbets' fans could be heard blocks away. For instance, at 521 Montgomery Street, just three blocks from Ebbets Field, Marty Feuerman could hear the crack of the bat and the resultant cheer from the park from his second-floor bedroom window. Feuerman was 24 in 1955, in his junior year at medical school on his way to becoming an opthalmologist. He was living on Welfare Island — now better known as Roosevelt Island — at Metropolitan Hospital. But during the summer, he'd return home on weekends.

The Feuerman home was a typical postwar two-family house; Marty and his parents lived upstairs, his grandmother downstairs. During spring and fall, Marty was torn between his Tilden High School homework and the Dodger games on the Emerson table model radio. "I'll never forget trying to study with the radio on," Feuerman recalls. "You could hear the roar through the open window and I'd run to turn the radio on. I sat in my bedroom and tried — but didn't often succeed — to do my homework. My homework got done, I just did the work later."

Because of his home's proximity to the park, Feuerman always felt Ebbets Field was in the primarily Jewish Crown Heights — "the only neighborhood that never had a Christmas tree or Christmas lights," Feuerman points out with some pride. "You didn't go to high school together, not to dances, you didn't live near each other," he says of neighboring ethnic groups. "But Ebbets Field was the great equalizer. When you went there, it was Us against Them."

Once Feuerman started his collegiate career at Brooklyn College, he made a deal with his father, a Manhattan-based attorney, to attend Sunday games against the Cardinals. "The Cardinals were the class of the league,"

These four Brooks bombers set a club record by smacking six homers in an 11–8 thrashing of the Braves on Wednesday night, June 1. Robinson, Reese and Campy, who each smacked one, support Snider, who blasted three and drove in six runs.

Feuerman explains. "I know the Giants were the hated rivals, but the Cardinals were the team to beat."

On Sunday, June 6, father and son bought a pair of general admission tickets, sat in the grandstand, ate hot dogs, and watched Robinson crack a game-winning, two-run homer in the bottom of the ninth for a 5-4 victory over the Cards. The home run was sweet for Robinson, still mired in what seemed like a season-long slump and playing in his first game after sitting out three games with a sore ankle.

The Dodgers continued to win in front of sparse crowds. The next day, only 4,500 showed up for Podres' five-hit shutout. Newk beat the Reds for his 10th straight decision without a loss the next night before only 7,700. One of them was nine-year-old Lenny Shostack. Lenny lived in the tough Brownsville section of Brooklyn, home of Abe Stark's store and former base of Louis "Lepke" Buchalter's Murder Inc. Lenny's dad was a painter who often worked at Ebbets Field. Papa Shostack would often come home from work with souvenirs from stadium workers who'd dislodge balls hit into the Bulova clock atop the scoreboard. "They'd say, 'This is one Gil Hodges hit or Duke Snider,' " Lenny remembers. "It was never autographed, but they knew who'd hit it in the clock. I used to toss them around, play with my friends. 'My father got it from Ebbets Field,' I used to say. 'Somebody gave it to him.' "

43

On this Wednesday night, Lenny didn't have to qualify his explanation about a ball he'd gotten from Ebbets Field. Father and son Shostack attended the game with a family friend, a local politico, and his sixteen-year-old daughter. Through his connections, Lenny's dad procured first row box seats on the third base line. Suddenly, a foul ball veered toward the group. "My father leaped right over and grabbed the ball," Shostack crows.

After the game, lefty pitcher Tom Lasorda was sent down to Montreal to make room on the roster for Koufax, returning from the disabled list after recovering from his ankle injuries. The next day, Bavasi sold Joe Black to the Reds for $15,000 and the familiar player-to-be-named-later.

Newcombe finally lost a game, snapping his 10-game streak, in the first game of a doubleheader on June 12. But after Podres tossed a seven-hitter in Wrigley Field, the first game of a long western road swing, the Brooks stood at 44-13, a .772 winning percentage, and had moved out to an 11½-game lead in the NL race. Snider led the majors in homers with 20 and RBI with 63 and was fifth in batting at .322. It was to be the apex of the regular season for both slugger and team.

The best hitters in the NL, not playing in New York: Ernie Banks of the Cubs,

AN INFIRMARY GROWS IN BROOKLYN

For the remainder of the summer, Alston would be forced to juggle a roster that spent more time in the trainer's room and in doctors' offices than on the field. The only pitcher who remained healthy was being cheered not for his fastball or curve, but his bat.

Newcombe's unbeaten streak, like that of the team's, had been a lucky combination of good pitching and great Dodger hitting, especially his own. On June 18, Newk won his 11th game on a seven-hitter, 12-1 against the Cardinals in St. Louis. Still asking for the rosin bag after each pitch, he also slammed his fifth homer, a two-run job to start the Dodger scoring in the third. He now needed just one homer to tie the NL record for homers in a season by a pitcher.

A couple of days later, Newcombe finally revealed to reporters the story behind the rosin bag. "Back in 1949, my first year with the Dodgers, a bat slipped out of my hand in Ebbets Field and struck a woman in the stands," Newcombe related. "They sued me and the club for $3,500. It was settled only a few days ago for $250 and, as I understand it, I'm to pay half. So, ever since then, I've been extra careful to make sure my hands are dry when I'm swinging a bat." Newcombe's belief that he owed half the settlement was mistaken. He had fallen prey to his prankster teammates, who had carried an off-handed remark by Bavasi to its extreme. But not even the clubhouse kibitzers or the media could distract Newk; by June 26, he was hitting .451, which led Alston to use his righty pitcher as his top left-handed pinch-hitter.

Stan Musial of the Cardinals,

Loes, however, had a sore shoulder, and he was ordered by club doctor Harold "Doc" Wendler to rest. Both Podres and Meyer also complained of shoulder soreness. When Meyer tried to pitch, a collision at the plate landed him in traction with a fractured collarbone and a herniated disc. Erskine was suffering sharp pains in his right elbow that would plague him the rest of the season. The pitching shortage finally forced Alston to start his bonus baby, Koufax, on July 6. The injury-prone lefty surrendered just one run in five innings and gained his first major league victory, but pulled a rib cage muscle in the effort.

Hearing about the Dodger pitching woes, Preacher Roe, now running a supermarket in West Plains, Missouri, 250 miles from where the Brooks were playing in St. Louis, dropped by and threw batting practice, prompting speculation that he might end his short retirement if Loes' shoulder remained sore. "When I read that Cox [Roe's roommate for seven years] had quit," Roe kidded, "I decided that one member of our room should be in the game."

Metropolitan-area hospitals were not only hosting pitchers. Campy had incurred a painful five-inch cut on the inside of his right thigh while blocking the plate against bull-like Giant catcher Wes Westrum on May 28. He also suffered from bone spurs in his left knee, as well as a stiff shoulder, and still had some numbness in his left thumb. On June 28, in front of more than 30,000, the largest crowd of the season at Ebbets Field, this pile of infirmities finally forced Campy to the bench, where he would remain until after the All-Star game. Which was too bad, since Campy was the leading vote-getter in the All-Star game voting.

The catching situation became more serious three days later. Campy's backup, Rube Walker, was run over by Willie Mays and would miss three days. This left the team with only one catcher, 35-year-old bullpen catcher Dixie Howell. Inevitably, Howell sprained his ankle two days before the All-Star game. A groin pull by Reese and Robinson's latest incapacitation — loose cartilage in his sore left knee — gave the team its 28th injury. Healthy-as-a-horse Hodges was the only Dodger not to miss a game.

Podres, Loes, and Spooner all returned by July 4, the traditional halfway point of the season; Erskine came back a few days later. According to baseball lore, the team in first place by Independence Day will win the pennant, and the Dodgers still held a 12½ game lead. But with the memory of 1951 still in mind, Alston was not comfortable. The manager canceled batting practice to dress down his indifferent and sloppy first-place team. After the Dodgers swept the Phillies in Philadelphia, Brooklyn had played half its games and stood at 55-22, a record that projected to an improbable 110-44 season.

All-Star manager Durocher named Newcombe to the pitching staff and Hodges to the reserves, both joining starter Snider on the NL team. Leo ironically passed over his protege, Reese, who would miss his first All-Star game since 1946. Durocher also bypassed Newk and his 14-1 record and gave Robin

and Ted Kluszewski of the Reds.

Roberts (13-7) the starting honors. Musial's homer in the 12th inning won the game for the Nationals in Milwaukee on July 12. Newk pitched a scoreless seventh, Snider went hitless, and Hodges got hit by a pitch in his only at bat.

A week into the second half, the injuries continued. Campy caught a foul tip on his left pinky and was forced back to the bench for a couple more days, Robinson popped a knee, an injury that would keep him sidelined for a month, and Amoros pulled a leg muscle. Snider was taking penicillin for the flu and a viral infection, but was still playing.

Injuries continued to plague the mound corps as well. Erskine was still out, as was Meyer, and Podres' arm hurt so much he couldn't sleep. The question was whether to call up some help from the minors. "We'll know in the next day or so just where we stand," Bavasi stated.

THE ROOKIES

On July 14, 1955, Congress authorized the first federal air pollution study. On July 18, Howard Hughes, aviator and billionaire eccentric, sold the RKO movie company to a television mogul, opening the door for endless old movies on TV. On the same day, Walt Disney opened his dream amusement park, Disneyland, in Anaheim, California, just south of Los Angeles. In Geneva, President Eisenhower, British Prime Minister Anthony Eden, French Premier Edgar Faure, and Soviet Premier N. A. Bulganin, along with the First Secretary of the Communist Party Nikita Khrushchev, started a five-day meeting to discuss German reunification and general improvement of East-West relations.

Three days earlier, Newcombe won his 15th, 12-3, against St. Louis, and smacked his NL record-tying sixth homer, leaving him three shy of the 24-year-old major league mark of nine by the Indians' Wes Ferrell.

The same day, Bavasi made his pitching move, calling up bespectacled Don Bessent and 6'4" Roger Craig. The two rookie hurlers had a great deal in common, in addition to being potential savers: both were from the South, born six months apart in the winter of 1931, both were signed in 1950, both were married with a daughter, and both were righties with a nasty sinker.

Bessent and Craig made their debuts two days later, July 17, in a Sunday doubleheader against the Reds in Brooklyn. A witness at the pair's debut was Chuck Camp, the 12-year-old son of a grocer from Morristown, New Jersey.

Chuck's father had moved to Morristown from Brooklyn before the war, but fought the traffic on weekends to go to Ebbets Field in the family's 1954 Chevy Belair. Because Chuck was a big Gil Hodges fan, his dad always got box seats behind first base. "I played first base in little league," Camp recalls. "I had a Gil Hodges glove, I had a Gil Hodges ball, I had a Gil Hodges everything." Camp also remembers his seat location because the Dodger Sym-Phony was based directly behind him. "They wandered around, but they came back to one place."

The rookies: Don Bessent and Roger Craig (below, being congratulated by Alston afterward) beat the Reds in both ends of a July 17 Ebbets Field doubleheader.

Camp's hero didn't disappoint on this day. Hodges homered in the first game as Craig threw a complete-game, three-hit 6-2 victory. Bessent, however, needed a little more help in his debut, combining with Ed Roebuck for an 8-5 victory. But the doubleheader sweep wasn't Camp's only memory. "I dreaded leaving Ebbets Field because the traffic jams were horrendous," he says.

To boost attendance, the club initiated some marketing gimmicks. The next night, a Buick donated by Mid-County Buick was won in a "guess the attendance" contest. Peter Girolyme of 1572 Coleman Avenue, Jack Stein of 2816 W. 30th Street, and G. A. Ferris of 4302 Ridge Boulevard, all guessed the correct number, but Girolyme won a tie-breaking baseball quiz held at home plate and drove the car home. Stein received $500 and Ferris $250. Entertainment between games of a doubleheader later that week was provided by a precision dance team of 24 girls from Las Vegas, Nevada, High School.

The biggest promotional event of the season, however, was a tribute to Brooklyn's beloved captain, Pee Wee Reese. On Friday evening, July 22, the Dodgers held an enormous birthday party for their shortstop, who would turn 36 the next day, which drew the season's largest crowd, 33,003.

In pregame ceremonies, Reese stood at home plate with his wife Dorothy and their 11-year-old daughter Barbara, and received tributes and $10,000 worth of gifts from 50 different presenters. Speeches were made by baseball commissioner Ford Frick, former Dodger GM Lee MacPhail, borough president John Cashmore, and Brooklyn congressman Francis Dorn. Reese was surprised by the appearance of his mom, who had told him she couldn't make it. Telegrams arrived from Governor Averell Harriman of New York, Kentucky

Senator Alben Barkley and Governor Lawrence W. Wetherby, Louisville Mayor Andrew Broadus, and Vice President Richard M. Nixon.

Then MCs Vin Scully and Happy Felton steered an emotional Reese to the microphone. "When I came to Brooklyn in 1940 I was a scared kid." He paused, then swallowed hard. "To tell you the truth, I'm twice as scared right now." He went on to thank all the fans who had been so wonderful to him.

At the end of the fifth inning, two giant birthday cakes were wheeled out to home plate. At a signal from Felton, all the lights in the park were turned off and every fan either lit a match or a cigarette lighter and sang "Happy Birthday To You." At 11:05, it was announced that a congratulatory telegram had been received from the nation's first fan, President Eisenhower.

Pee Wee celebrated his night in style, banging out a pair of doubles to key a 12-hit attack, but it was Furillo's eighth-inning three-run homer that gave the Brooks an 8-4 victory over the Braves. The victory stretched the Dodger lead to 14½ games, their largest of the season.

Injuries dogged the Dodgers, reaching even into the broadcast booth. "Happy" Felton, master of the Knothole Gang and WOR-TV's pregame show, was kayoed by a line drive before a game. Outfielder Sandy Amoros entered Long Island College Hospital for treatment of his chronic sore back. He had batted just four times since July 15, and his average had dropped from .342 to .267. One patchwork lineup had only Reese and Snider in their regular positions. After one game, Bavasi walked into the clubhouse, tossed his coconut straw hat onto Alston's desk, and asked loudly enough for all to hear, "Anybody else injured today?" "Yeah," came a voice from a far corner, "Jake Pitler. His leg hurts." Someone else cracked, "Aw, to hell with him," as laughter broke out at the reference to the popular coach.

By early August, Alston finally got some good news. Robinson was ready to return. Snider ended an 0-for-16 slump with his 36th homer. Erskine, Podres, Spooner, and Meyer were all due back within the week. With his two rookies a combined 6-0 and the reliable Newcombe now 18-1, Alston soon would have too many pitchers.

JERSEY CITY AND POINTS WEST

Cleveland, Chicago, and the Yankees were all tied for first place in the American League during the first week of August. White Sox General Manager Frank Lane, in optimistic preparation for his team winning the AL pennant, noted that the aging Brooks could no longer hit good pitchers. "I never could," Reese quipped in response. Other Dodgers sarcastically wondered where the White Sox would get good pitching. But O'Malley wasn't yet ready to claim victory, despite his team's huge lead. "Remember 1951?" O'Malley reminded everyone.

Pee Wee Reese Night, July 22.

But both the press and the players felt they had the race well in hand. This allowed the press to cover other stories. Would the Duke, whose 38 home runs put him seven games ahead of Babe Ruth's 1927 pace for 60 homers, break the record? And how would Alston set his Series pitching rotation? He threatened to award starting World Series spots to his effective rookie tandem "unless Erskine and Loes come back and show me they're better than the kids — and I'm beginning to wonder a little." Alston decided not to gamble on overworking his veterans and ordered Loes to rest his arm. To prepare for the Series, Alston took a day off to scout a Yankees-Red Sox game at the Stadium.

The front office was busy finishing plans for Old Timers Day on August 14 by locating the oldest living Dodger — John Herman Doscher Jr., 75, of Ridgefield Park, New Jersey, a lefty pitcher for the Brooks from 1903-06 who had won one game. During the break between games of the Sunday double-header split with Philadelphia, Commisioner Frick introduced old-timers sitting in the stands, including Babe Herman, Whitlow Wyatt, Otto Miller, Nap

Rucker, Art Dede, Leon Cadore — and, at her usual center field bleacher perch, Hilda Chester.

One hot item was the mid-August announcement that the Dodgers had been given permission to play seven games in Roosevelt Stadium in Jersey City in 1956. O'Malley was quick to point out that this did not necessarily presage the move of the Dodgers to another city, although that was not out of the question, either.

"We plan to play almost all our home games at Ebbets Field in 1956 and 1957," O'Malley asserted. "But we'll have to have a new stadium shortly thereafter." O'Malley reeled off the litany of Ebbets Field's inadequacies. It held 32,111 and had parking room for only 700 cars. Attendance had declined steadily, despite the team's success, from a 1947 peak of 1,807,528, a then-NL record, to 1,020,531 in 1954, a drop of 150,000 from 1953. O'Malley did not expect the 1955 juggernaut to draw even a million fans.

"Our fans require a modern stadium, with greater comforts, shorter walks, no posts, absolute protection from inclement weather, convenient rest rooms, and a self-selection first-come, first-serve method of buying tickets," O'Malley stated. "We will consider other locations only if we are finally unsuccessful in our ambition to build in Brooklyn. But our stockholders are prepared to build in Brooklyn and not elsewhere."

O'Malley's veiled threat to "consider other locations" prompted immediate reaction from city officials. Mayor Wagner intoned that he was "very anxious to keep the Brooklyn Dodgers in New York City" and said he'd confer with O'Malley. All-powerful bridge and road builder Robert Moses publicly voiced his enthusiastic support for finding the Dodgers a new New York City home. But, behind closed doors, the man who built every major freeway and public beach on and every toll bridge and tunnel to Long Island, acted conversely. He considered spectator sports a waste of time and money — money he could use to build more roads, bridges and parks — and ordered his political apostles on varying city bodies to vote against key Dodger-related appro-

priations. To keep up appearances, Cashmore publicly pleaded for and received a token $50,000 allocation from the Moses-controlled New York City Board of Estimate to survey a new ballpark site.

O'Malley may or may not have understood — or cared — about Moses' political opposition; he may even have counted on it. In all events, he began to shift the onus of action from himself to the city. "To clear up any misconceptions, I would like to make it plain that we are not going into this with our hats in our hands," O'Malley assured nervous tax payers. "We are — and have been for some time — ready, willing, and able to purchase the land and pay the costs of building a new stadium for the Dodgers. We have six million dollars available for this purpose if an adequate site can be made available. But we do need help from the city to acquire the necessary land at a reasonable price." O'Malley then added without explanation that Ebbets Field had to be sold by 1958.

Fan reaction was predictable. "The Dodgers belong in Brooklyn," asserted Bill Murray of 681 Lafayette Street, a tugboat inspector. "When my wife read the news last night, you should have heard her. 'They can't do this to us. We Brooklyn fans ought to get together and stage a demonstration.'" Another fan noted that Brooklyn has "the cream of baseball and now they want to take it away from us. And don't forget Brooklyn is the best of the five boroughs and deserves the best."

Other fans in front of Brooklyn Borough Hall expressed their opinions. Theresa Pearl of 3133 Brighton Street, a legal stenographer, demanded that "they should make every effort to keep the Dodgers here. I'll bet St. Louis is sorry it lost the Browns and Philadelphia the Athletics. Things like that are bad for business." Joe Stzyvinski, a messenger, of 524 Chauncey Street, was more direct: "It's a dirty trick to pull a stunt like this. Sure, I know they need a new ballpark. But they're just too cheap to get one here in Brooklyn." "Maybe Ebbets Field isn't the best ballpark in the world," noted another, speaking for all. "But a lot of Brooklyn people have been going there for a lot of years — and liking it — win, lose, or draw."

The press tracked O'Malley's Machiavellian moves as if reporting a chess match. And while the Dodger president was hosting a luncheon for Jersey City officials at the Hotel Bossert on August 22, the Dodger offices became the target of inquiries from a dozen different localities — including Staten Island — offering a haven for the Dodgers. The day of the luncheon, the Los Angeles City Council sanctioned an official reconnaissance. LA city council-

Mike Harkavy and Tom Tassone watched the Dodgers break out of a late-season funk with a fury. Campy swings and smacks his 28th homer of the season...

woman Rosalind Wyman invited both O'Malley and Giant owner Horace Stoneham to Los Angeles in late September.

At games, whenever a fly ball was hit, the cynics in the press box chanted "Home run in Jersey City!" In the lead paragraph of one article, columnist Dick Young referred to the team as the "Jersey City Dodgers."

DOG DAYS

On August 20, President Eisenhower declared Connecticut, Massachusetts, Pennsylvania, South Carolina, and parts of New Jersey and Rhode Island disaster areas as a result of major flooding. He should have included Brooklyn.

Distracted by press speculation about a repeat of 1951's fiasco as well as a possible move, the Dodgers had lost 9 of 13 and seen their lead shrink from 16½ to 11 games. And they were still in danger of running out of bandages. Podres had been slammed on the foot by a line drive and had a swollen left instep. Newcombe was having trouble winning his 19th — he hadn't won a game in almost a month. On his fifth try at number 19, he pulled a shoulder muscle and had to leave the game. Although he was not expected to miss a start, Newk joined Erskine, Loes, Spooner, Podres, and Meyer, who were all still questionable. The corseted Amoros was playing, but he was visibly slowed and not hitting. Robinson's trick knee was responding to treatment — "I'll be fit for the World Series," he reported — but Alston didn't want to rush things. Rather than subject Robinson to the rigors of playing third, Alston planned to use him in left field to give Amoros a rest.

Even the healthy players were struggling. Roebuck had given up nine homers in his last 10 innings of work. Hodges hadn't homered since August 5. And Snider was mired in another slump. By the time the last-place Phils swept them in Ebbets Field on August 21, he was 0 for his last 12 and had driven in only two runs in 12 days. Reds slugger Ted Kluszewski and Cub shortstop Ernie Banks had passed him in the home run derby. Although he was tied with Mays for third in the RBI race with 111, he now had little chance of top-

ping Campy's club record of 142 RBI. "I don't feel strong," Snider moaned, still recovering from his mid-July flu bout. Alston reasoned that "anybody who hit as good as Duke did for as long as he did is entitled to a little slump." Alston used the same rationale to explain the team's dismal performance in August. "Damn it, they've been playing such good ball all season, you've got to expect a little slump. They're not complacent, not acting as though they've got it won." Former Dodger great Zack Wheat added his own vote of confidence, calling the 1955 Dodgers the best Dodger team of all time.

On August 24, the team played up to Wheat's assessment, thrashing the Cubs 9-4. Hodges finally homered, one of four Dodger round-trippers. With Gilliam suffering a slight headache, Robinson led off for the first time since 1948. "That's the first easy game we've had in a couple of weeks," sighed a relieved Alston. "And believe me, it was a treat."

The game was also a treat for Tommy Tassone and his buddy Mike Harkavy, who lived across the street from each other in the Canarsie section of Brooklyn, Tommy at 1631 E. 48th Street, Mike at 1634. Both attended P.S. 203, both collected baseball cards, and both were Dodger fans. They had to be Dodger fans — Gil Hodges' wife's uncle lived down the street. For seven-year-old boys, even this slight association with a real Dodger imbued their block with a touch of big league class and entitled them to certain bragging rights in the school yard, especially when the soft-spoken first baseman came to call on his relative.

Tommy and Mike exhibited the dedication to their team typical of seven-year-olds. They clipped boxscores and slavishly pasted them into scrapbooks. Going to real games, however, was rare. Their hard-working dads were just too busy to take them.

Finally, the boys' moms decided to treat their young sons to a Wednesday day game. The group found themselves sitting on the third base side of the protective screen strung up behind home plate. Foul balls hit onto the top of the netting would roll down, tip off the brace wire, and fall into the hands of a ball boy. The two boys watched in wonder as a long-limbed man in his 30s stood on the guard rail and, reaching around, snagged a ball as it tipped off the brace wire.

The man snagged a second foul off the bat of Amoros in this fashion. He then turned to a surprised Tommy, said, "Here you go," and dropped the perfect white sphere into the boy's hands.

A major league baseball — an actual ball actually touched by the actual bat, glove, and hands of actual major leaguers. This was a great souvenir to an adult, but was an object of awe and wonder to a seven-year-old. "We played with it until the cover fell off," Tassone remembers. "At first we would only walk around with it and play with another ball. Then when it got its first scuff mark, we started to loosen up. For a while we only played with it on the grass. But after that, we played with it all the time." Each took turns guarding it at night. While watching Dodger games on the Harkavys' 15-inch RCA Victor TV, they displayed it like a talisman.

Tommy's mom Audrey was an attractive and religious Brooklyn home-maker who ran a reading school in her home. She and Mike's mom, Harriet, often played housework hooky together at Ebbets Field while their husbands were working. They loved the team and baseball, but the Dodger players also functioned as examples to her children. When Robinson broke the colorline in 1947, she decried Dixie Walker's racism as "un-Christian-like." She held up Robinson as a role model to Tommy, who played basketball at the local Y. "Look at what Robinson does," she would lecture. "Look at how he hustles. Never stop hustling. That's what you have to do." When she wanted some-

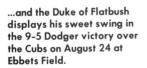
...and the Duke of Flatbush displays his sweet swing in the 9–5 Dodger victory over the Cubs on August 24 at Ebbets Field.

thing done quickly, she wanted it done "as fast as Jack Robinson."

Audrey came to be a Dodger fan naturally — she had a tendency to root for the underdog, and to be a bit contrary. Her mother was a Yankee fan, and her father and her best friend were Giant fans. As a 14-year-old, she went to Dodger-Giant games and felt natural rooting for "those bums," even though she herself hated the nickname. "I would never allow that word to be used in my house," she says. "Nobody was ever a bum."

That opinion wasn't shared around Ebbets Field in the final humid days of August, however. After the Dodgers impressive victory over the Cubs, the team lost three straight to the last-place Reds, starting with an embarrassing doubleheader sweep on Thursday. Snider was actually booed, both for his lack of hitting and for some angry remarks he had made at the initial negative fan reaction to his slump. Brooklyn fans "don't deserve a pennant" and are the "worst" fans anywhere, he had been quoted as saying.

After a second day of booing, he half-apologized for his remarks. "There are some good Brooklyn fans, but maybe there are more bad ones. In a way I'm sort of sorry I popped off. But it wasn't altogether the booing they gave when I didn't hit. Boos weren't the only thing they tossed at me. They threw other things at me from the stands in center field. Once something nicked my shoulder and when I looked at the ground, what d'ya think it was? A beer can opener. That's not funny." Duke was clearly distracted. One explanation was that his wife Beverly was expecting their baby back home in Los Angeles.

Alston reflected that "the fans here are as loyal as anywhere. They may boo a little more, but they cheer more, too. It's like a closely knit family where brothers may fight, but just let an outsider pick on either of them, and they'll both gang up on him. That's how the Brooklyn fans are."

The pitching shortage forced Alston to once again start his bonus baby, Koufax, on Saturday, August 28. The 19-year-old responded with a brilliant complete-game, two-hit, 7-0 victory. Koufax struck out a league season-high 14, including veteran Gus Bell four times, and held the Reds hitless from two out in the first to two out in the ninth.

Koufax's performance broke the slump. Furillo's two-run homer gave him a career-high 22. Robinson's two-run shot was his first since June 28. Spooner threw a six-hitter at the Cardinals the next day, his first complete game in 11 starts. For the first time in a week, there were more cheers than jeers for Snider. On Monday, the team's third young lefty, Podres, won, and Snider broke out of his slump, slamming a three-run homer, his first homer since August 5. Robinson stole home for the 18th time in his career on the front end of a triple steal, and said he felt as good as he had when he was a rookie.

The next day, Newcombe finally won his 19th, an 8-6 decision over the second place Braves, which featured the 40th homer from a suddenly rejuvenated Snider. It was his sixth straight hit over two games and gave him his third straight 40-plus homer season. Campy's three RBI gave him 100 for the season.

"In the spring, I said this was the most determined club I had ever seen," Robinson told reporters after the game. "Everybody on it seemed driven by a desire to make up for last year's flop. Sure enough, that's what happened. We got off winning. But lately, that spirit seemed gone. People were talking about how we were losing a length one day, and a half length the next, and you never can tell when something like that will begin to get a club down. Now I think the fellows have that old determination back again. They want to get this thing over with as soon as possible."

The victory reduced the Dodger magic number to 12 — any combination of Dodger wins and Brave losses would give Brooklyn another National League pennant.

CHAPTER III

THE WORLD SERIES

Pennant

The hazy, lazy, crazy days of the summer of '55 were over, Labor Day weekend approached, and it was soon back to school.

Brooklyn may have been the Borough of Churches and Manhattan's bedroom community, but it was also the world's most diverse school district. And being in school during a pennant race and World Series made boys and girls very itchy. Series games were almost considered a legitimate excuse to play hooky. Almost.

Dolores Fahey lived on 11th Avenue with her parents, five sisters, and one brother, what their primarily Italian neighbors called "Irishes." In 1955, she was attending St. John Villa Academy, a parochial school on Staten Island that attracted Brooklyn's Irish Catholic community. Dolores would take the ferry every morning and review the previous day's Dodger results with her friends, Joannie Maloney and Mary Muldoon, to be ready for the Italian girls at school who were all Yankee fans. "All we did was argue with them," recalls Dolores, now Mrs. Whitelaw. "They thought the Yankees were the greatest and we thought the Dodgers were the greatest. To make your argument hold water, you had to learn who was batting what."

Dolores had plenty of ammunition as the 1955-56 school year started. Her team was riding the crest of their last hot streak of the season. Beginning with Koufax's gem, the Dodgers won 12 of 13, including the first eight games in September. During the string, the team also played its last memorable game of the regular season, the opener of a doubleheader against the Phillies on September 5. The more than 15,000 that were turned away at Ebbets Field missed seeing Newk finally win his 20th and smack his seventh homer to set a new National league record for pitchers. In the sixth inning, Zimmer, Reese, and Snider bashed solo homers, for Duke his 42d. It marked the first time all season the Brooklyn bombers tallied three round trippers in an inning.

Outside Ebbets Field, sometime during the 1950s.

The rest of the Dodger hitters seemed to be peaking at the same time. Campy had five homers and 14 RBI during the winning streak and raised his average to .331, good for second in the league in his attempt to become only the third catcher to win a batting crown. Duke was batting over .500 for the week and was at .316 for the season. Furillo, who had sagged to .270 in mid-July, was now back up to .314.

In Milwaukee two days later, Loes won his first game in a month. The following day, September 8, the Dodgers ended their hot streak in style with a 10-2 victory, clinching the earliest pennant in National League history, beating their own 1953 mark by four days. But even though they had delivered on their preseason promise and brought the NL championship back to Brooklyn, there was no on-field demonstration. The players merely trotted off the field as if it were just another victory.

Things were a little different in the clubhouse, though. Campy, already dressed because of his first inning removal after getting hit on the wrist, led the reception committee. He was puffing on a cigar and dragging from a bottle of beer. "Where's the champagne?" Newk wanted to know. "I'm not giving you any," Campy replied. "You can't stop me," Newk replied. "Don't let this wrist fool you," Campy laughed. But there was no champagne, only beer and crackers. The bubbly was waiting at the party to be held at a downtown Milwaukee restaurant.

Seemingly immune to the shenanigans was O'Malley, who walked around the locker room shaking hands and answering questions about one of their prospective World Series opponents. "I want to beat the Yankees. We have to beat the Yankees once some time or another and this ought to be the time."

Silky-voiced Vin Scully informs the Brooklyn faithful that, once again, their boys are in the World Series.

The NL champions on their pennant-winning parade through Brooklyn on September 16.

The knowledge that the job wasn't yet complete, combined with the inevitability of the Dodgers' clinching, resulted in a rather muted reaction back in Brooklyn. Earlier in the day, City Council President Abe Stark cut a garland of bagels to officially open a Dodgerville Room at Juniors Restaurant on DeKalb Avenue and the Flatbush Avenue Extension downtown. But when the Dodgers won, there was hardly a peep — for some reason, the room was filled with Giant fans, and the bartender was a Yankee fan. Carl Sanders, the owner of the Dodger Cafe at 24 DeKalb Avenue, said, "This is it!" and announced plans to change the mural behind the bar from the 1947 team to the 1955 edition. However, his only customers at clinching time, a little after 6 pm, were a young couple. "The fellow is a Giant fan and the girl is a Dodger fan," he whispered. "Don't bring this up now." Along Flatbush Avenue, traffic cops said they were too busy to care one way or the other. The Brooklyn celebration would have to wait until the end of the road swing.

When the Dodgers arrived at LaGuardia's Marine Terminal at 11:50pm on September 15 aboard their charter flight, the several hundred fans present noticed the legend "Brooklyn Dodgers, 1955 National League Champions" painted on the DC-4's tail. The next day, the players rode in open cars along the two-mile route from Grand Army Plaza up Flatbush and Fulton avenues lined with an estimated 300,000 fans, to Borough Plaza where they were greeted by another 20,000 faithful. The appreciative fans had all pitched in and bought each player a gift — a four-piece silver service — as they might have for any of their Brooklyn neighbors celebrating an auspicious occasion. The Dodgers thanked their fans later that evening by beating the Giants at Ebbets Field, snapping a five-game slide.

But not everything was roses as the team watched the American League race between the Yankees, Cleveland, and Chicago. For one thing, Newk felt ill. He didn't have a temperature, but he complained that "my back aches, my legs ache, and my eyes ache." He was diagnosed with a slight intestinal virus and ordered to bed. Podres' ailment was a bit more serious. During the last

homestand, he'd been shagging flies and accidentally ran into the batting cage, which was being wheeled back under the grandstand. After ignoring the pain for a week and suffering a 9-0 drubbing by the lowly Reds, he was discovered to have a severe muscle pull, not the suspected cracked rib. But he would still be out for a week, making him questionable for the Series. The rest of the pitching staff wasn't all that healthy, either with Erskine, Loes, and Spooner all suffering from varying elbow and shoulder woes.

A few days later, Newcombe reported that his appetite had returned, but he still felt weak. Spooner, however, had aches and chills. It was suspected that he had contracted whatever virus Newcombe had had.

On September 19, the Duchess of Flatbush gave her Duke a 29th birthday present, an 8-pound baby boy, Kurt Brian Snider. By this time, the team was coasting to the season's end, hoping to get one more shot at the Yankees.

THE YANKEES AND OTHER DISTRACTIONS

Larry King, née Zeiger, couldn't figure out his buddy, Herbie Cohen. In Brooklyn, being a Giant fan was unbelievable. But, as the royal opposition, the Giants could at least be respected. The Giants were, after all, a blue-collar team with great players, just like the Dodgers. Rooting for the Giants, even if you were from Brooklyn, may have been dangerous, but was at least an honest affectation.

But Herbie Cohen was a Yankee fan and, in Brooklyn — or in any working-class, immigrant community — being a Yankee fan was just plain screwy. Sure, the Yankees were good — great, in fact. In the 34 years from 1921 to 1954, the Bronx Bombers won 20 American League pennants and 16 world championships. In the post war era, the Yanks won the World Series in 1947, 1949, 1950, 1951, 1952, and 1953.

There was no sports team more respected or feared than the Yankees. Rooting for the Yankees was like rooting for Goliath against David, like rooting for the iceberg against the Titanic, like rooting for the spider over a fly. The Yankees represented the class and sophistication that Manhattan had always flaunted over Brooklyn. "The Yankees were the America that we were denied," King explains.

The Yankees, White Sox, and Indians entered September separated by just a half game. The Labor Day weekend, however, marked the return of Yankee sparkplug Billy Martin, the hero of the 1953 Series. Army Corporal Martin had spent the season on duty at Fort Collins in Colorado Springs and was granted a 30-day furlough to help his team down the stretch.

Two weeks after Martin returned, the Yankees were two games back of Cleveland. On September 16, the Yankees got some good news and some bad news. They pulled into a first-place tie by beating the Red Sox in the Bronx, but lost Mickey Mantle. While trying to leg-out a bunt, the slugger pulled a muscle

One of several team pictures of the 1955 National League champions, taken September 16 before a game against the Giants. Sitting with the year is Charlie DiGiovanna, the batboy; the seated row (left to right): Shuba, Zimmer, coach Joe Becker, coach Jake Pitler, Alston, coach Billy Herman, Reese, Dixie Howell, Amoros, Campanella; middle row: clubhouse man John Griffen, Erskine, Koufax, traveling secretary Lee Scott (in suit), Craig, Newcombe, Spooner, Hoak, Furillo, Kellert, Doc Wendler; back row: Meyer, Gilliam, Loes, Labine, Hodges, Roebuck, Bessent, Snider, Podres, Walker, Robinson.

in his right thigh. The next day the Yanks moved into first place for good.

On Friday, September 23, the Yankees beat the Red Sox, 3-2, in the second game of a doubleheader in Boston to clinch the American League pennant. Although this was front-page news in the New York Times, there were bigger stories in what would be a busy week. For one thing, President Eisenhower, on vacation in Colorado, suffered a slight heart attack, which was later diagnosed as a coronary thrombosis. On the sports page, yet another Yankee pennant was dog-bites-man news, easily overshadowed by the sudden resignation of Leo Durocher as Giant manager.

The Dodgers closed out their season with a 4-0 victory over Pittsburgh, with four pitchers scattering eight hits. Podres pitched a perfect first two innings, but was tabbed only for bullpen action for the Series. Snider narrowly missed his club-record 43d homer when his 450-foot drive hit only halfway up the distant Forbes Field right field wall for a triple. Pirate manager Fred Haney, fired that day by Pittsburgh president Branch Rickey, pitched lefty Dick Littlefield for the final three innings to give the Dodger righty hitters some practice against similar lefty Yankee World Series starters Whitey Ford and Tommy Byrne. The Dodgers got five hits off Littlefield, but no runs.

In Boston, Mantle pinch-hit in both ends of the Yankees' season-ending doubleheader, seeking his 100th RBI for the season. Batting lefty in both appearances necessitated putting steady pressure on his injured right leg, and he was in obvious pain with each swing. He flied out twice, and didn't bother to run. "I feel okay right now," The Mick drawled, "and I sure hope I'll feel all right to start the Series."

PRELUDE

The Yankees finished 3½ games ahead of Cleveland at 96-55. The Dodgers finished 13½ games ahead of Milwaukee at 98-55, their second-best record ever, topped only by their 105-victory season in 1953. The Dodgers led the majors in every major offensive category, including homers with 201, only the third team in history to top 200. Among personal performances, Campy ended fourth in the league in batting at .318, Furillo was seventh at .314, and Snider was ninth at .309. The Duke led the majors in RBI with 136 and finished fourth in homers with 41. Every Dodger starting pitcher finished the season with a winning record, led by Newcombe's 20-5 mark, save Podres, who ended at 9-10.

These were the facts. But twice previously, a more impressive Dodger team entered the World Series against a statistically inferior Yankee team, only to fail. Daily News beat writer Dick Young vocalized the consensus reason: "I realize that a guy can find himself floating in the Gowanus Canal for less, but I'd rather be right than alive. I am the only one I can't lie to, and I tell myself

These five still have more than a day to wait for the Ebbets Field ticket office to open at 8 pm on Monday, September 26. John Barr (far left) of 366 Second St. had camped out since Friday and planned to take his wife and kids; joining John are George Schneider, Edward Connelly, Don Martin (standing), and Jack Martin.

that the Dodgers just don't have the pitching to win with."

The odds-makers agreed. Based on past experience and a position-by-position comparison, the Broadway bookies installed the Yankees as 6-7 favorites, 18-10 for both the opener and the Series.

Most other people just subscribed to varying forms of the Yankee jinx theory. Joe DiMaggio, on a visit to Rome, decided to act more like a Viennese shrink. The Dodgers, DiMaggio diagnosed, were "crazy mixed-up kids with a deep psychological block — they can't beat the Yankees in the World Series. I guess the only thing that can cure them is a brain-washing. It has gotten so bad with them in Brooklyn that they can't even say the word 'Yankees.' It's always 'those blankety-blank lucky Yankees' — to put it politely."

That sort of comment wasn't unexpected coming from a former opponent. What was surprising was a similar view from a former Dodger — Billy Cox, speaking from his home in Newport, Pennsylvania. "They always fold in the Series," the former third baseman noted of his former team. "Maybe it will be different if some other team than the Yankees take it in the AL, but if it's the Yankees — well, they're the Dodger jinx."

Cox's former mates didn't take kindly to the jibing from the

Pennsylvania peanut gallery. "That doesn't speak well for him," Snider said angrily. "He was always on those teams with us. He must be off his rocker." "He's just sore because he was traded away," Furillo reasoned. "Where does he come off, anyway? When he looks in the mirror, he can say to himself: 'There's a real foldup.' "

Reese spoke for his teammates who, like real champions, were actually happy to have another shot at their annual fall tormentors. "I think most of us wanted the Yankees to win the American League pennant just so we could play them. I know as far as I'm concerned, this may be my last World Series as a player. And I want to go out of this game beating the Yankees."

Audrey Tassone was like all Dodger fans. She didn't pay attention to the opinions of newspaper columnists, gamblers, or former players. The Dodgers would win, period. When she moved with her family to E. 48th Street in Brooklyn, she had discovered that her neighbor, Jack Harkavy, was a Yankee fan. In 1952 and 1953, she and Jack made friendly $2 bets on the Series. Immediately following the final out of each, she strode across the street and dutifully paid up. Jack would refuse to accept, but Audrey insisted. He and the Yankees had won fair and square.

Manager Alston instructs his players at an Ebbets Field workout on Monday, September 26. From left, Snider, Campanella, Hoak, Newcombe, Zimmer, Gilliam, Reese, Hodges and Robinson. Furillo was still out with the flu bug that had been working its way through the Dodger clubhouse and missed both the practice and the photo op.

As late summer turned to fall, Audrey saw the Dodger-Yankee rematch as an opportunity to earn back half her losses, as well as a chance to avenge the team's previous four Series losses. "It was like bedlam in Flatbush," she said as the World Series neared. "It was just a phenomenal coming together. I mean, people smiled, thumbs up." If there was any talk of another possible Dodger loss, she dismissed it as "idiocy." "No, this was our real chance."

She might have reconsidered if she knew about the flu rampaging through the Dodger clubhouse. Possible rain predicted for Wednesday's Series opener didn't make Alston any happier, except for the hope that a rainout might give his staff an extra day for rest and recovery.

The Yankees, on the other hand, had a deep and well-rested staff: lefties Whitey Ford (18-7, 2.63 ERA), who led the AL in victories, and Tommy Byrne (16-5, 3.15), and righties, "Bullet" Bob Turley (17-13, 3.06) and Don Larsen (9-2, 3.06).

Alston, as he had in spring training, was reconsidering his starting eight. He named the versatile but weak-armed Gilliam his left fielder, relegating the still-limping, and still-slumping Amoros to the bench. The even lighter-hitting Zimmer was assigned Gilliam's regular second base job.

Amoros wasn't the only Dodger unhappy about this move. "Gilliam should be asked to report to spring training with the pitchers so he can teach them how he throws his change-up," quipped one Dodger on Gilliam's notoriously weak throws. In spacious Yankee Stadium, where the first two Series games would be played, Gilliam's arm in left could signal a Yankee base-running bonanza. "Amoros can throw better than Gilliam," Alston conceded, "but Junior makes up for it by charging ground balls and handling them cleaner." Alston further rationalized his choice by noting that Amoros hit a disappointing .247 for the season. Gilliam wasn't much better at .249, but he was a switch-hitter.

Starting Gilliam or Amoros didn't make much difference with the oddsmakers and sportswriters. In the mano-a-mano matchups, the Yankees held an edge, especially on the pitching side:

THE MATCHUPS

1B: GIL HODGES VS. BILL "MOOSE" SKOWRON/JOE COLLINS:
Hodges was the superior fielder, but was a streaky and unpredictable Series hitter (e.g., his hitless streak in the '52 Series). Skowron was the better hitter, Collins the better fielder of the Yankee tandem. EDGE: EVEN

2B: DON ZIMMER/JUNIOR GILLIAM VS. BILLY MARTIN:
Between the Brooks, Zimmer had slightly more power and a better arm, Gilliam was better with the glove. Martin was potentially a better hitter and fielder than either Dodger. EDGE: YANKEES

3B: JACKIE ROBINSON/DON HOAK VS. GIL MCDOUGALD:
Robinson was injury prone and past his prime; Hoak was young and inexperienced. McDougald was better defensively and had had a superior offensive regular season than either of the two Dodgers.   EDGE: YANKEES

SS: PEE WEE REESE VS. PHIL RIZZUTO:
Reese was a better hitter and had a stronger arm than Rizzuto, who had the better glove.   EDGE: DODGERS

LF: JUNIOR GILLIAM/SANDY AMOROS VS. IRV NOREN/ELSTON HOWARD:
This position was weak for both teams; both used non-outfielders to fill in — infielder Gilliam for the Dodgers, and catcher Howard for the Yankees. Overall, the Yankee tandem hit better and had more experience.
                                                                                                                      EDGE: YANKEES

CF: DUKE SNIDER VS. MICKEY MANTLE/NOREN/BOB CERV:
Without a healthy Mantle, Duke ruled.   EDGE: DODGERS

Waiting for tickets before Game 1 at Yankee Stadium: On September 27, Ralph J. Belcore enjoys a snack, and Charles M. Kierst smokes a cigar.

The following day Mrs. Mabel Thompson (center), who obviously thinks her Dodgers will sweep, gets jinxed by Yankee fans Mrs. John Hull (left) and Mrs. Alice Baker (right).

RF: CARL FURILLO VS. HANK BAUER:

Furillo was a better hitter, had a rifle arm, and played the Ebbets Field right field wall smoother than Louis "Satchmo" Armstrong played the trumpet. EDGE: DODGERS

C: ROY CAMPANELLA VS. YOGI BERRA:

Campy was the superior defensive catcher, but always had trouble hitting in Yankee Stadium. Each catcher was a threat in his own park, but there were four possible games at Yankee Stadium, only three in Brooklyn. EDGE: EVEN

P: NEWCOMBE, LOES, ERSKINE, SPOONER, PODRES, CRAIG VS. FORD, BYRNE, TURLEY, LARSEN, BOB GRIM:

The Yankee staff was deeper and healthier — an even more critical factor in this Series, which would be played in consecutive games with no days off, as was the custom when little or no travel between locales was needed. On the negative side, none of the Yankee prospective starters had ever beaten the Dodgers. But on the Dodger side, Newcombe always had bad Series luck, and the rest of the Dodger staff was a question mark. EDGE: YANKEES

MANAGER: WALTER ALSTON VS. CASEY STENGEL:

Alston was a Series rookie; Stengel was the architect of five straight world champion Yankee teams from 1947-53. EDGE: YANKEES

At 8 pm on Monday, September 26, there were already 4,500 fans circling Ebbets Field to begin the competition for the 34,000 available tickets for the possible three games in Brooklyn. First in line was father of seven John Barr of 366 Second Street, who had camped out under the ticket window Friday night. "There'll be trouble," he predicted, "if the kids want to go, and maybe my wife will decide she should go too."

The circle was actually two converging lines, one starting at McKeever Place, one on Sullivan Place. Way back in one of these lines was Mortin Silver, a Yankee fan from Troy, New York, who nonetheless carried pennants for both teams. He had arrived at 8 o'clock Sunday morning. "This will be my 17th Series," he explained. "I always come down when they play in New York." He already had purchased SRO tickets at Yankee Stadium Saturday. "Just walked right up and bought them. No waiting, like here." By midnight, all the games in Brooklyn were sold out.

On Tuesday, both teams worked out at the other's park. Snider, who hadn't homered since Labor Day, hit one into the stadium's right field seats. "I think I found the range again," the Duke of Flatbush ominously intoned.

YANKEE STADIUM

The World Series was a nationwide phenomenon, despite the purely local tone it had had since the war. At Wabash College in Crawfordsville, Indiana, for instance, there was at least one student rooting for Brooklyn. Robert Wedgeworth was the first and only black at the small Midwestern liberal arts school, and was feeling a little out of place among the midwestern white undergrads. It was the Dodgers that kept him connected to home and family. "I couldn't relate to my classmates about how we felt about this team," Wedgeworth remembers. "I really couldn't share that feeling with anybody."

At 8 o'clock on Wednesday morning, 14,000 unreserved bleacher seats went on sale at Yankee Stadium. Mike Sharff, together with 50 frat buddies from New York University and Brooklyn College, and other "normal" Dodger nuts from his Flatbush neighborhood, joined 1,500 others who had been on line since before midnight Monday. "The kind of nut who stayed on line like we did was much more likely to be a Brooklyn Dodger nut than a Yankee nut," Sharff recollects. This overnight vigil was less nutty than it was water-logged; a pelting rainstorm had held the first-game bleacher line down. Most of the seats went unsold until the sun peeked through the clouds at around 10 that morning. Sharff, like most Dodger fans, ended up in the right field bleachers for most of the games, two or three rows from the stadium's back wall.

In front of Dave Kaminer's sixth-grade class at the Stevenson School on Stevenson Boulevard in New Rochelle, New York, stood teacher Hadassah K.

Fraternizing with the enemy: Yankee starter Whitey Ford poses with Dodger Game 1 starter Newcombe (top), and Dodgers Snider and Reese consult with Yankee center fielder Mickey Mantle (below).

Holmes, a tough old bird, "older than the world," Kaminer recalls, "the toughest of customers, right out of central casting."

Like millions of school kids, daytime World Series bouts meant an increased fidget factor as 1 pm game time approached. "I'm dying because I don't think there's a chance in the world that I will be able to listen to the game," says Kaminer. "I begged my parents to let me stay home sick, but they wouldn't let me."

But old birds aren't always so tough, as Kaminer discovered after lunch. "She says 'settle down' and goes over to the cupboard on the right side of the room. I can still see her do it. She pulls out a radio the size of a toaster, turns it on, and says, 'We're gonna listen to the World Series.' She lights up a cigarette, leans back in her chair, and says 'Let's go Dodgers!' " Old Hadassah K. Holmes was human after all.

"We couldn't believe it," Kaminer says, still sounding stunned. "Hadassah let us listen to all the games in the World Series. That was a joyous time."

Kaminer was lucky. Most school kids — and working adults — would have to wait for periodic updates from those lucky enough to be able to listen or watch. Elliott Goldstein, for instance, was taking tap and ballet lessons at Max Goldfarb's studios on Broadway between 53d and 54th Streets in Manhattan, above the theater where Ed Sullivan's Sunday night TV show was broadcast.

Goldstein had just graduated from the Professional Children's School and was commuting daily on the D Train to Manhattan from his home at 1644 49th Street in Boro Park in Brooklyn. His dance sessions lasted from 3 to 6 pm, which meant that he could squeeze in some radio time for each of the games before his classes. During classes, he would sneak up to Goldfarb's offices on the third floor or to the sixth floor where Mable Horsey, an elderly blues singer and teacher, ran a studio, to catch snippets of the game on the radio.

"I had to try not to allow those games to interfere with my studies," notes Goldstein, who would later change his name to Gould and become an actor in such popular films as "M*A*S*H". "I went because the guy who ran Mable's studio was an elderly black man, and I felt very comfortable up there. I could listen with people who also identified with the Dodgers. Mable, I'm sure, was rooting for the Dodgers, too. Hey, that was Jackie's team."

Back in the Bronx, luminaries including Governor Harriman and singing cowboy Roy Rogers shed superfluous outer garments in the suddenly sun-drenched liquid air. Flags were unfurled, color guards turned heel-toe, and the teams were introduced, aligned along the baselines. After a short prayer for President Eisenhower's speedy recovery from his mild heart attack, the national anthem was sung. Former ballplayer Mayor Robert F. Wagner threw out the ceremonial first pitch, a high hard one to Berra. It was probably the most effective pitch of the day for either side.

Elston Howard trots toward first on his way around the bases after his second-inning two-run homer off Newcombe tied Game 1, 2-2.

The first real pitch of the Series was a high and tight fastball from Ford to Gilliam for a called strike. On Ford's next delivery, Gilliam hit a tapper back to the mound. Reese followed with the Series' first hit, a line single to left, but was left stranded. The spectacular regular season, just days past, was now old news. The quest had begun.

The Brooks struck first in their half of the second. Leading off, Furillo, shaking off the effects of his lingering cold, reached out and slapped a liner off Ford's first offering down the right field line. It bounced off the top of the short concrete wall and into the bleachers behind the 296-foot mark for a solo homer. Now that the spell had been broken, Robinson followed an out by Hodges with a triple into Yankee Stadium's left-center field gorge. Stengel

73

pulled the infield in to cut off the run at the plate, an odd move so early in the game. Zimmer crossed up the strategy by blooping an RBI single into shallow right field that probably would have been caught for an out had second baseman Martin been in his usual position. The Dodgers led 2-0.

The Dodgers didn't have much time to enjoy the lead, however. In the bottom of the inning, Yankee first baseman Joe Collins walked with one out. Elston Howard, batting for the first time in a World Series, pulled a hanging curveball and curled a two-run homer around the left field foul pole to knot the score at 2.

Snider gave the lead back to Brooklyn when he led off the top of the third with a mammoth homer into the stadium's third deck in right field. The Yankees tied it immediately in their half of the third when Ford, who had walked to open the inning, scored on a ground out by Noren. The Dodgers threatened to take the lead back again in the fourth, but with two on, Martin turned a Reese hot smash into a double play. It was the turning point of the game.

Collins led off the Yankee fourth. A month earlier, mired in a horrible slump, Collins had borrowed Mantle's bat. Voila, no more slump. His hot hitting continued in the Series. He knocked Newk's second pitch into the lower seats in right field to snap the 3-3 tie. In the sixth, after Berra's one-out single to right, Collins cracked another long drive to right-center field, over Snider's head, the auxiliary scoreboard, and the fence, to give the Bombers a 6-3 lead.

Unfortunately for Newk, the Yanks weren't done in the inning. Slap-hitter Martin surprised Gilliam by driving a long triple off the left field auxiliary scoreboard. Alston had seen enough and replaced Newk with Bessent. Eddie Robinson pinch-hit for Rizzuto when Martin took off for home. Sliding feet first, he appeared to have reached the plate before a diving Campy landed on top of him. But home plate umpire Bill Summers had a rear view, not the camera's side angle, and thumbed an astonished Martin out. As the two players disentangled, Martin threw an elbow at Campy's face. A serious but satisfied Campy simply headed for the dugout, leaving Martin seething.

Ford settled down and kept the Dodgers from threatening until the eighth. With one out, Furillo singled. Robinson followed with a smash down to third that glanced off the glove of a backtracking McDougald and dribbled behind the base, allowing both runners to move up. Zimmer's sacrifice fly to right scored Furillo and Robinson moved to third. With Kellert pinch-hitting for Bessent, Robbie started dancing as far as 30 feet down the line. When he finally took off, Berra seemed ready. The ball beat the aging Robinson to the plate, but Summers apparently believed that his toe had caught the plate before Berra applied the tag and called him safe. Berra jumped up and down, uncharacteristically apoplectic. But the call stood and the Dodgers were down by just a run.

The steal, ill-advised from a strategic point of view with the Dodgers trailing by two runs, was a calculated move by Robinson. He later explained it

Duke Snider leaps in vain as Joe Collins' second homer of the game gives the Yankees a 6-3 lead in Game 1.

In the sixth inning of Game 1,
Billy Martin tripled then tried
to steal home. Although
Martin appeared to have
beaten the play, umpire Bill
Summers thumbed him out.

Disgusted, Martin tried to dis-entangle himself from Campy by throwing an elbow (left). Eddie Robinson (#36) turns and walks back to the dugout, los-ing a chance to pinch hit for Rizzuto.

Yogi, however, disagreed with ump Bill Summer's safe call.

Jackie Robinson slides into Berra's tag on his daring steal of home in the eighth inning of Game 1 in his attempt to spur his mates on to a comeback.

was primarily motivational in nature, an attempt to awaken his mates from their lethargy. It didn't work that day. Furillo ruined his perfect 3-for-3 day by waving at a high outside fastball from reliever Bob Grim for strike three to end the game, a 6-5 Yankee victory.

Robinson lunges in vain after Bauer's ground single through the hole in the first inning of Game 2 as Reese at shortstop and pitcher Billy Loes look on.

"You don't like to lose that first one, of course," Alston philosophized afterward. "But none of the boys sound disheartened. They're still confident and so am I."

The matchups for Game Two on a brilliant sunny autumn afternoon were sore-armed Loes and 35-year-old Byrne. Loes was surprisingly effective for three innings. So was the crafty Byrne, mixing breaking pitches with an occasional fastball, and destroying for the second straight day the Dodgers' legendary domination of left-handed hurlers.

Once again, the Dodgers posted the first score and should have had more. Reese led off the top of the fourth with a double. Snider then sent a drive into the right field corner. Reese scored easily, but Duke thought a fan had touched the ball and eased around first, on his way to a presumed grounds rule double. When he realized the ball was in play, he shifted into high, but right fielder Howard, subbing for Bauer who had pulled his right thigh muscle sliding in the first inning, threw him out at second.

Again, the Yankees gave their foes precious little time to enjoy the tiny lead. With two out and no one on in the bottom of the fourth, Berra singled to right-center. Collins walked on four pitches. Howard drove in Berra with a line single to right to tie the score. Martin singled through the hole into left to knock in Collins and give the Yanks a 2-1 lead. Stengel, smelling a big inning, sent up Eddie Robinson to pinch-hit for Rizzuto and Loes hit him in the upper back with a pitch to load the bases, Jerry Coleman going in to pinch-run. The next batter, Byrne, was a good hitting pitcher, and he made the most of his RBI opportunity. He whistled a fastball past Loes' head up the middle into center field, a single good for two runs. That ended the afternoon for Loes.

The Dodgers managed to scare up one more tally in the fifth when Gilliam's single scored Robinson. But the crafty Byrne became only the second lefthander to toss a complete game victory over the Dodgers in 1955, surrendering just five hits in the 4-2 Yankee triumph. "I was disappointed in our hitters," Alston understated. "I thought they'd hit that lefthander better than they did."

In fact, the Brooks would have to hit better, period. Alston discussed some possible lineup changes for Game Three, including Amoros in left and Gilliam in place of Zimmer at second, "to get another lefthanded hitter in the lineup," to face Yankee righty "Bullet" Bob Turley.

BACK TO BROOKLYN

Audrey Tassone assessed the Dodger chances: "I thought they'd come back, I really did," she said, ignoring the fact that it had been 34 years since a team had come back to win a Series after being down two games to none. "I thought that they were as frustrated as we all were and that they would do something spectacular, maybe crazy, but spectacular. I didn't care how they

Brooklyn fans wait for the Ebbets Field box office to open to buy standing room tickets for Game 3. Dolores Byrne and her boyfriend Pat Brady got to be first on line by showing up at 11:30 pm on September 29 (right), and Fay Hatch uses a bagel instead of a crystal ball to predict a Dodger victory (far right).

Campy crosses the plate after his first hit of the series, a two-run homer in the first inning of Game 3. He is being greeted by Dodger batboy Charlie DiGiovanna, on-deck hitter Furillo (#6), and Reese (#1), who led off the inning with a walk and had scored ahead of his catcher.

won. I'm not one for going in spikes-high, I don't think that's very nice, but I was willing to accept it whatever way it happened." She backed up her words with action; she and Harriet Harkavy attended Game Three at Ebbets Field on Friday afternoon, September 30.

The choice of starting pitcher for the Dodgers came as a surprise. Alston needed a lefty to curb the Yank lefty power duo of Berra and Collins. It was Erskine's turn, but Alston gave the ball to the peach-fuzzed Podres, celebrating his 23rd birthday.

Podres almost wasn't on the World Series roster. He had lost much of his effectiveness since his painful encounter with the batting cage in August. But Podres' two scoreless innings in the season finale against Pittsburgh convinced Alston to keep the youngster around.

Keeping Podres on the roster was one thing. Starting him in a game the Dodgers absolutely, positively had to win was another. First, lefties never had much success at Ebbets Field; even Stengel had used his portsiders in roomier Yankee Stadium. Second, a stiff, 25-mile-per-hour wind was gusting to left, adding 10 feet to every fly hit by a righty batter. Third, Podres hadn't pitched a complete game since June 14. His last victory was August 29. In his previous decision, he was clobbered by the last place Reds, 9-0, on September 11. Finally, in his only other start against the Yankees, in Game Five of the 1953 classic, he gave up five runs and didn't finish the third inning.

Just as much a surprise was the pitcher whom Alston was bypassing —

Erskine. The classy and popular right-hander had started three games in the previous two Yankee-Dodger matches, and set a record of 14 strikeouts in the opening game of the 1953 Series. He was the Dodgers' senior hurler, and the most experienced one against the Yankees. But Erskine also had been smacked around in his last few appearances.

Podres was presented with an early lead. With one out in the first, Reese walked. Two outs later, Campy planted a not-so ballistic Turley fastball into the lower left field bleachers and the Dodgers led, 2-0.

As had been their habit, the Yankees immediately answered. To bolster the lineup against lefty Podres, and because Bauer was still unable to play, Stengel was forced to put a gimpy Mantle into the lineup. The gamble paid off when Mantle pounded a fat Podres offering 395 feet into the center field bleachers. But Mantle was noticeably in pain as he hobbled around the bases.

Podres was clearly shook by the malevolence of Mantle's solo blast. He surrendered a double to Skowron. With two out, Rizzuto was due up with Turley on deck. Alston strolled to the mound to discuss walking the shortstop to get to the weak-hitting pitcher. They decided to pitch to the Scooter. It was the wrong move. The Yankee sprite hit a one-hop zinger to left. Campy caught Amoros' relay five feet up the line just as Skowron reached him. Campy sidestepped and applied a sweeping two-handed tag. The massive Moose led with his elbow, knocking the ball from Campy's glove. As the ball soared toward the roof of the Dodger dugout, Skowron danced to the plate and toed it with the tying run.

Meanwhile, Rizzuto took second on the throw and didn't stop as he saw the ball sail away. The ball, however, took a Brooklyn bounce. Instead of landing in play, which would have allowed Rizzuto to score, it dribbled off the concrete dugout roof and into a vacant TV camera nook. The ball was declared dead and Rizzuto was sent back to third. He died there as Turley grounded out to end the inning.

The Brooks took advantage of the lucky bounce in their half of the second. With one out, Robinson again showed the way by singling sharply up the middle. An errant Turley delivery pegged Amoros in his right thigh. Podres popped a bunt down the third base line, but English on the ball spun it away from Turley's glove and all hands were safe. The Dodgers had three runners on, but unlike the Vance-Fewster-Herman convention at third base in 1926, it was one Dodger to each base.

With Robbie dancing farther off third with every pitch, the rattled Turley walked Gilliam on five pitches to force in the tie-breaking run. Stengel, mindful of Turley's sudden bursts of wildness, decided to bring in "Plowboy" Tom Morgan. But Morgan promptly walked Reese on four pitches to force Amoros home with the Dodgers fourth run. Morgan steadied himself and got Snider to hit into a force play at the plate, and Campy lined out to Martin to end the threat.

Morgan didn't stay steady, however. Gilliam singled to left to open the

But Campy had his troubles the following inning when husky Yankee first baseman Moose Skowron elbowed the ball loose and scored in the second inning to tie the game, 2-2.

fourth. After Reese popped out, Snider walked. Campy drove in Gilliam with a single to left, sending Snider to third. Snider scored when Furillo fouled out to give the home team a 6-2 lead.

Podres, meanwhile, tossed changeup after changeup to set up his fastball, keeping the Yankees off balance. His only other anxious inning was the sixth, when Mantle stepped up with McDougald on second and Berra on first. Alston had Bessent warming up and visited Podres on the mound ready to make a switch. But Alston left without Podres. The youthful birthday boy, having attended the school of hard knocks on Mantle's first at-bat, abandoned changeups and fastballs and threw nothing but curves. Podres induced the crippled Mick to ground into an easy double play.

The Yanks did break through for a run in the seventh when pinch-hitter

Yankee reliever Tom Morgan has just walked Reese to force in the Dodgers' second run of the second inning of Game 3. That's Amoros about to score to give the Dodgers a 4-2 lead, with Podres heading to third and Gilliam to second.

Andy Carey tripled in Rizzuto. The Brooks came right back, however, after the seventh-inning stretch. With one out, Robinson doubled into the left-center field gap off reliever Tom Sturdivant. Robbie made a purposeful wide turn at second and Howard took the bait. When the inexperienced Yankee left fielder unleashed a throw to second, Robinson dashed safely to third. Amoros singled past Skowron and a drawn-in infield to score Robinson. Podres' sacrifice attempt forced Amoros at second. Gilliam walked. Reese followed with a single through the middle to score Podres with the final run of the game for an 8-3 margin.

While munching on birthday cake after the game, Podres was approached by Alston. "He told me if there was going to be a seventh game, that I was going to be the pitcher," Podres later recalled. "That was a hell of a confidence booster for me, coming off the type of year I'd had."

News of the Dodger victory was muted, however, by other events. The 24-year-old actor James Dean was killed when he lost control of his sports car on a California curve. After his death, the release of "Rebel Without a Cause" sealed his legend. And while one legend died, another was being born. The number-one country single during the World Series was a remake of "Mystery Train" by a young singer from Tupelo, Mississippi, named Elvis Presley.

In Denver, a recovering President Eisenhower took back the reigns of executive power by signing a couple of minor State Department documents from his Fitzsimons Army Hospital bed. And in Princeton, New Jersey, noted geodesic dome guru Buckminster Fuller, retained by O'Malley to design a new stadium, revealed plans for a circular domed park to replace Ebbets Field.

Game Four featured the delayed matchup between Erskine and Larsen,

The birthday boy at work. On his 23d birthday, Podres finished off the Yankees, holding on for the 8-3 victory in Game 3.

Amoros scores the first Dodger run of Game 4 after Gilliam's double in the third inning to cut the Yankee lead to 2-1.

Campy (#39) is greeted in the Dodger dugout by his mates after smacking a homer in the fourth inning to cut the Yankee lead in Game 4 to 3-2.

which turned out to be anticlimactic. McDougald, the second Yankee batter of the game, smashed an Erskine offering 375 feet over the Brooklyn Union Gas sign in left-center to give the Bombers a 1-0 lead. In the second, Collins walked, was sacrificed to second, advanced to third on a ground out, and scored when Rizzuto's grounder eluded a diving Reese. The Dodgers got one back in the third when Amoros, who had walked, slid in ahead of the relay throw from left field after Gilliam smacked a hit-and-run double.

Berra opened the fourth with a single and Collins walked again, ending Erskine's afternoon. Berra took third on a Bessent pitch in the dirt and scored when Martin's broken bat bloop dropped over Gilliam's head into shallow right for a 3-1 Yankee lead.

Campy got a run back when he led off the fourth with a homer over the Michael's & Co. Furniture sign in left. Furillo followed with an infield hit and scored ahead of Hodges, who reached out and poked an opposite-field homer over Abe Stark's sign in right center to give the Dodgers a 4-3 lead.

Gilliam helped run Larsen out of the game in the fifth. He walked to lead off the inning, and took second when Larsen bounced his first pitch to Reese. When Larsen threw a second pitch out of the strike zone, Stengel quickly brought in Johnny Kucks. Reese grounded to Skowron for a seemingly easy out. But Kucks was slow off the mound and Reese beat the pitcher to the bag for a single, Gilliam moving to third. Kucks made another mistake, a fat pitch to Snider that the Duke promptly turned on and sent 100 feet over the right field screen into Bedford Avenue to give the home team a 7-3 edge. Labine pitched the final 4⅓ to help the Brooks hold on to win, 8-5, and tie the Series at two games each.

After the game, no one was more disgusted at Erskine's poor performance than Erskine himself, who told Alston to remove him from any of his future Series pitching plans for the good of the team. The Dodgers lost another starter when Newk's shoulder stiffened up. After Spooner had spent several innings warming up in Game Four, Alston was left with only one rested pitcher for Game Five — rookie Craig, the least experienced pitcher ever to start a World Series game. He would be opposed by Bob Grim, Stengel's bullpen ace forced into a starting role as a result of the Yankees skipper's having to use multiple pitchers over the previous two games. Stengel was saving lefty Ford for Yankee Stadium before coming back with Byrne for a possible Game Seven.

As the 2 pm game time approached, the sky was cloudy. The gray weather didn't depress the crowd, however. An Ebbets Field World Series record 36,796 jammed into the tiny park. They didn't go away disappointed. In the second, Amoros smacked a two-run shot into Bedford Avenue. Snider hit two into Bedford, one in the third and another, longer drive in the fifth. The second shot caromed off a garage door and into the waiting hands of a 10-year-old girl, one of many youngsters armed with radios stationed behind the right field wall waiting for just such an opportunity. The two homers gave Snider four in the

Two batters later, after Furillo (#6) singled, Hodges put the Dodgers ahead for good, 4-3, with a two-run opposite field homer. Dodger batboy Charlie DiGiovanna is appropriately joyous, Hodges typically stoic.

Dodger rookie hurler Roger Craig pitches out of the second inning of Game 5. He'd just walked Collins and Eddie Robinson, but got Martin, Rizzuto and Grim out without letting the ball out of the infield.

Series, making him the only player to hit that many in two separate World Series. It also gave him nine career Series homers, a National League record.

In the meantime, Craig was unflappable in the face of Yankee power, more so since Mantle and an equally hobbled Bauer sat on the bench. Mixing mostly breaking balls with an occasional fastball, Craig limited the Yanks to six hits in six innings. In the seventh, Cerv, batting for Grim, smashed a homer deep into the left field seats, the 100th Yankee Series homer, to cut the Dodger lead to 4-2. After Craig passed Howard, Alston quickly lifted his rookie hurler in favor of the reliable veteran Labine, who promptly induced Noren to bounce into a sweet Hodges-to-Reese-to-Hodges double play.

In the eighth, Labine gave up Yankee Series homer 101 to Berra to trim the Brooks' lead to one run. But in the Dodger half of the inning, off Turley in relief, Robinson's seeing-eye single dribbled past Rizzuto and scored Furillo with an insurance run for a 5-3 final. The three-game sweep at Ebbets Field marked the first time

Amoros has just given Craig and the Dodgers a 2-0 lead after homering to right in the second inning of Game 5. Hodges (#14), who scored ahead of him, and batboy DiGiovanna help him across the plate.

Homage is paid to the Duke of Flatbush, returning to the Dodger dugout after giving his team a 3-0 lead with a homer into Bedford Avenue.

Clem Labine (left) and Roger Craig bask after beating the Yankees in Game 5.

in Series history that a team had won three games after losing the first two.

To say that the Yankees were glad to be back in the Bronx would be putting it mildly. The Bombers had been complaining about the "cheap" homers the Dodgers had smacked at the Flatbush bandbox. "Only Snider's second clout would have been a homer in our park," moaned crybaby Collins. "I know we've had the same chances they've had, but it's tough to lose a game by two runs when three of these came on cheap flies."

Alston decided that a healthy Spooner was better than a questionable Newcombe for Game Six. The Yankees were ready and waiting to ambush the young lefty. To open the game, Spooner walked Rizzuto, who stole second when Martin struck out. Spooner then walked McDougald. Berra Baltimore-chopped a single over Spooner's head and by Gilliam at second to score Rizzuto. Bauer, starting for the first time since Game Two, singled past Robinson to score McDougald. Skowron then ended Spooner's short after-noon with an opposite-field three-run homer into the right field seats to give the Bombers a 5-0 lead. The homer was the 17th of the Series, tying the Series record the two teams had set two years earlier.

That bulge was plenty for Ford. The crafty lefty effortlessly scattered four hits and struck out eight in a complete game. The only flaw in his gem was an RBI single past a lunging Rizzuto in the fourth by Furillo that scored Reese with the Brooks lone run. The 5-1 Yankee victory set up the final showdown for the next day, Tuesday, October 4.

CHAPTER IV

BUMS NO MORE

Game Seven

Bob Genalo was in the Catskills, in Smallwood, New York, with his wife, sister-in-law, brother-in-law, and one-year-old, Bob Jr. "It's really a shame," Genalo recalls, "but this brother-in-law was a Giant fan, you know, which is what brothers-in-law should be."

The family went for a nature walk, but Genalo veered off and ended up in a local rustic tavern to watch the game. "I was the only Dodger fan in the bar. They were all Yankee fans — not a human being in the crowd." And being from Brooklyn, Genalo wasn't shy about his allegiance, either. "Every Dodger fan rooted out loud, I don't care where they were. You could be the only person in the world. It was constant arguing all day long with Yankee fans. Yankee fans have an arrogant, pompous way about them, you know, like they're the greatest and nobody's better. They keep calling on all these statistics as if they really have some meaning. They never believed that the Yankees could ever lose."

Chuck Camp was attending class at the Vail School in Morristown. During the Series, he would get into arguments with classmate John Klausner, a Yankee fan whose father was executive vice president of a local department store. "Very corporate, yeah. He'd always needle me because the Yankees would win every year. They had the best center fielder, and they had the best shortstop, and they had the best catcher, and the best first baseman, and the best everything. And the best pitchers. He was convinced that the Dodgers would lose again."

Camp's teachers crammed all the work they could get in that morning. Then, amazingly, the game was piped in over the PA system, which was supplemented by huge portable radios that some of the students had schlepped in. "And then we'd do workbooks and math problems and things like that" with the game going on in the background.

Fans lining up outside Ebbets Field during the 1950s.

Elliott Gould decided to take the day off from his tap and ballet lessons. Down the street from the Broadway studios was a newsreel theater where a communal 24-inch television had been set up. "It cost like 40 or 60 cents to get in," Gould recalls. "I remember when I went to Grand Central Station to meet my father when he came home from World War II, and this was something like that. Just hundreds of people standing, shoulder to shoulder, watching the last innings of the 1955 World Series. There were some Yankees fans, but I didn't know Yankee fans and I didn't know Giant fans. I only knew Dodger fans."

Radios and televisions were blaring and glaring all over Brooklyn. Lenny Shostack also was in school that day, at P.S. 156 on Sutter Avenue. "Some kids had radios in the class. And I remember the teacher told them to shut them off."

The adult Harkavys and the Tassones were watching on their respective TV sets, waiting for the boys to get home from school. Audrey laid in a supply of Schaefer beer, even though the Tassones were teetotalers. "We had to buy Schaefer because they sponsored the game," Audrey reasoned. "There should be some product loyalty." Once the game started and the boys got home, the Tassones didn't take time to eat or drink or move. "If the telephone rang," Audrey says, "I sent the kids to answer it. We were glued."

Not surprisingly, Marine Park Bakery owner Stan Keizerstein also halted his day's labors after lunch. "Are you kidding?" he asks incredulously. "The seventh game of the World Series, the Dodgers and the Yankees, you think I'm gonna work? I told my father, I said, 'Pop, I'll see you later.' At that time of the day, I would be working behind the counter. My mother came down and she worked a little bit for me."

Keizerstein repaired upstairs to the apartment to watch the game on a console Admiral with a tiny 10-inch screen, but was too nervous to sit still. "At that time I smoked and I don't think I smoked any cigarette very far. I was like a father waiting for the birth of his child. I remember I turned the TV off and turned it back on every time there was a tense situation. I couldn't watch it."

Podres' family in Witherbee, New York, a tiny mining town of 1,500 nestled in the orchard-pocked Adirondacks near bucolic Lake Champlain, didn't have a television set. Joseph Podres, a miner for Republic Steel, drove with his brother to Yankee Stadium to see his son pitch in person. Mrs. Podres and her other four children went to the home of her brother to watch the deciding game.

Like most 23-year-olds, Podres was oblivious to history and his place in it. "If you had a guy who won 20 games pitching the seventh game of the World Series, there'd be more pressure on him going in because he's supposed to win," Podres later explained. "Me, there was no pressure on me. If I'da lost this, they'd have said, 'Well, who expected him to beat the Yankees two straight?'" Opposing Podres was Game Two winner Byrne.

Both teams would have to do without key components. Mantle had been demoted to pinch-hitting after Game Four. But if the Yankees were with-

Third base ump Lee Ballanfant calls out Rizzuto, who has just slid into Gil McDougald's grounder to end the Yankee threat in the third inning of Game 7. Don Hoak, playing third for a hobbled Robinson, looks a bit stunned by the lucky break.

out their heart, the Dodgers were missing their soul. Robinson had aggravated his Achilles' tendon. Willing but unable, feeling old and frustrated, Robinson was forced to watch Don Hoak play third in Game Seven. All things considered, no one was surprised when the odds-makers installed the Yankees, playing in their own park behind an experienced hurler, as favorites to beat Brooklyn yet again.

Inside the cavernous concrete stadium, thoroughbred jockey Eddie Arcaro took the day off from the races to witness the climactic contest. Unbeaten heavyweight boxing champion Rocky Marciano was back at the Bronx edifice as a spectator in Yankee co-owner Dan Topping's box. Two weeks previous, Marciano, who would retire unbeaten early in 1956, made his final title defense, a ninth-round KO of Archie Moore.

As usual, Mike Sharff had settled with his buddies into the back of the right field bleachers. "I would guess that the bleachers, unlike the rest of the stadium, were probably evenly divided. There were fanatics on both sides. There was a lot of verbal taunting back and forth. They gave us more crap than we gave them because they really had more firepower from all the years they had won."

There were mostly Yankee fans in Section 11 of the upper deck above the first base line where 35-year-old Union City, New Jersey-resident Pat DeClemente was sitting. "We got to the game about a half-hour before it started," remembers DeClemente, who traveled to Ebbets Field for about 20

games a year. "I'm not a screamer, but I would yell an exclamation of one sort or another — 'Good,' 'Atta boy.' I was very wound up, very nervous as the game went on." He wasn't any more or less nervous than any of the 62,000-plus fans in the stadium and the millions listening and watching in Brooklyn, the nation, and around the world.

Significantly, Alston made good on an earlier lineup change threat. He reinstalled Zimmer at second, shifted the weak-armed Gilliam to left field, and moved Amoros to the bench. Fortunately for the Dodgers, this was not a permanent arrangement.

Both Byrne and Podres gave early indications that the team's power surge of the first six games had fizzled. Rizzuto celebrated his record 52d World Series game by short-hopping Gilliam's high chopper in front of second and flinging the speedy Dodger left fielder out by a step for the first out in a 1-2-3 first. With a popping fastball and a change of pace dancing just enough to keep the Yankee sluggers off balance, Podres breezed through his own 1-2-3 first inning. It was obvious to both Podres and Campanella that the young left-hander had good stuff.

In the Yankee second, Podres stranded Skowron after the brawny first baseman bounced a two-out grounds-rule double into the right field stands. In the meantime, all the Dodgers could mount against Byrne in their first three attempts were a couple of harmless walks.

In the bottom of the third, Podres got into a two-out jam. He easily disposed of Howard and Byrne, then walked leadoff hitter Rizzuto on four pitches. Martin singled to right, giving the Yankees two on and two out. McDougald then chopped a slow bouncer up the third base line. Hoak was playing deep and had little hope of making a play on the ball, and it looked as if the bases would be loaded for the dangerous Berra. But before the sliding Rizzuto could reach third, the ball ricocheted off his leg for the third out.

Podres, frustrating the Yankees in Game 7.

A close call once again energized the Dodgers. After Byrne struck out Snider to open the fourth inning, Campanella pulled a shot that rattled around in the short left field corner. Howard had trouble picking up the careening ball and Campy camped on second with a double. It was his first and only hit in four games at Yankee Stadium during the Series, and the Dodgers' first hit off Byrne. Furillo then tapped a slow roller to short. While Rizzuto charged, bare-handed the ball, and underhanded it to first to nip Furillo, Campy crossed to third.

That brought up Hodges. With first base open, two out, and the weak-hitting Hoak due up next, Stengel scurried bow-legged to the mound for a strategy session. Do we walk the more dangerous Hodges and pitch to Hoak? Byrne had handled Hodges easily in a hitless three at bats in Game Two, striking him out to end the game.

Sitting in the bleachers, Sharff shivered. "Gil Hodges just was not the man you wanted up in clutch situations. As much as we loved him, he was not a clutch hitter. I remember his coming to the plate. I was prepared for a strikeout."

The Yankee brain trust must have agreed with the Dodger doomsayers and decided to pitch to Hodges. At first it looked like the right decision when Byrne slipped across two quick called strikes. But on the next pitch, Hodges muscled a too-close-to-take inside breaking ball over Rizzuto's frantic leap into short left field for a single to drive in Campy and give the Dodgers a 1-0 lead. Hoak grounded routinely to short to end the inning.

For Dodger fans, the run was no reason to get excited. Losing leads against the Yankees had become an annoying habit through the years. In Game Seven of their 1947 confrontation, for instance, Brooklyn had an early 2-0 lead, only to have the Bombers come back to take the game and the match.

Berra, stranded in the on-deck circle when Rizzuto slid into McDougald's slow roller to end the third, led off the Yankee fourth. Berra undercut a lazy opposite-field popup into no-man's-land in shallow left-center. Snider in center and Junior Gilliam in left each were playing deep and toward right out of respect for the powerful pull-hitting Yankee lefty. Both outfielders galloped in toward the spot where the ball would land, ending up standing close enough to shake hands. Both were looking up at the popup, both had their gloves down waiting for the other to yell, "I got it!" In predictable Dodger fashion, neither did, and the ball plopped between them for an embarrassing double.

Podres, with the poise of a veteran, just sniffed and turned to face the next batter. He induced Bauer to fly routinely to Furillo in right. Skowron grounded out to Zimmer for the second out. Cerv then popped a pitch up to almost the same spot where Berra had sliced his nine-iron shot to start the inning. Taking no chances, Reese, flailing his arms violently enough to take flight, yelled for the ball. He backed into short left to make the catch in front of his chastened outfielders.

THE CATCH

By this time, Podres was relying less on the changeup and went almost exclusively to spotting his fastball, and had little trouble over the next few innings. His teammates then went about getting him an insurance run in what would be the most eventful inning of the Series, the sixth.

Reese grounded a sharp single past Rizzuto into center field to lead off. Four-homer man Snider followed the orders of the conservative Alston and laid down a surprise sacrifice bunt to the right of the pitcher's mound. Byrne fielded the ball and flipped to the startled Skowron, who had started to charge but had stopped short five feet down the line from first. Moose caught the underhanded toss awkwardly and attempted to tag Snider in the chest as Duke went charging by him. Moose's body and left arm were spun around toward the pitcher's mound from the force of the tag, and the ball spurted out across the infield for an error.

With runners at first and second and none out, Campy dumped a more conventional sacrifice bunt to Byrne, moving Reese to third and Snider to second.

Stengel once again visited the mound. With Hodges on deck, he ordered Furillo intentionally walked. This would load the bases and set up a possible inning-ending double play. Once again, Sharff, in the bleachers, blanched. "I had no feeling of confidence whatsoever that he (Hodges) would ever get another run in."

Again, the Yankees agreed. Playing the righty/lefty percentage, Stengel brought in right-hander Grim to pitch to the right-handed Hodges. Grim got Hodges out, but it was on a deep fly to right-center that Cerv caught near the warning track. Reese tagged up and jogged home with the Dodgers' second run. Snider held second, Furillo first.

Alston wanted more. A Grim wild pitch moved Snider to third and Furillo to second. Hoak was then intentionally walked to get to the light-hitting Zimmer. Alston sent up George Shuba to pinch-hit, but he grounded out to Skowron at first to end the inning.

With Zimmer out of the game, Alston brought Gilliam back in from left field to play second. Rather than place the defensively shaky Shuba in the outfield, Alston summoned Amoros to take Gilliam's spot in left.

The pesky Martin led off the bottom of the sixth, working out a walk. McDougald bunted down third looking for a hit. Podres fielded the ball barehanded and whirled toward first, lofting an off-balance, ill-aimed rainbow across the diamond. Hodges casually caught the fly 10 feet north of the base as McDougald safely sped across the bag. Runners were now on first and second with none out, Berra at the plate.

The outfielders, including Amoros, dutifully shifted toward right field in anticipation of Berra pulling a pitch in that direction. Amoros, remembering Berra's dump shot in the fourth, played practically behind Reese in shallow left.

Berra stepped up, bat cocked high. Ball one, high and tight. Podres then tried to slip a fastball low and outside, tempting the notorious bad-ball hitter. Extending his arms to reach the outside pitch, Berra sliced the ball, up, up and away toward the left field corner.

It was a little after 3 pm when Berra hit the ball. Kids all over the East Coast were getting out of school, many listening to the game on radios they had brought with them and now were free to listen to. Many more were rushing home to catch what they could of the game on TV. "I just came home from school," says Shostack. "I was in the living room and my dad was home from work that day. He was ill. And my mother, who never cared for baseball, found the game interesting because the whole family was watching it. My sister was home also. I came home and I heard."

"You got on your bike, and you went like a crazy person, you drove the half mile home as fast as you could," Camp recalls. "I can distinctly remember, my father was home. I had to leave the room. I couldn't handle it. I left when Yogi was coming up. I went out into the kitchen, because the TV was in the living room. I didn't want to hear or know, because I knew, that was it. It was over. We lost again. Yogi would've done something, something was going to happen, and I just couldn't handle the pressure."

Inside the Stadium, Sharff had a problem. His back-row seats in the right field bleachers were at an angle that limited his view of the left field corner. He saw the ball being hit but, as the crowd jumped up, his view was completely blocked. But he had no doubt that the Dodgers were once again going to be foiled by last-second Yankee heroics. "We were convinced it was going to be a home run, because that's the way it always happened."

But Podres didn't share the fans' fatalistic opinion. "When Berra first hit it, I said to myself that it was an out. Then I saw the ball kept slicing. Amoros picked up the speed out there and I thought, 'Oh my God, is he going to get it?' " It was a question millions of people were asking during the succeeding, seemingly frozen, seconds.

Amoros had been crouched more than 150 feet from the Stadium's left field line. At the crack of the bat, Amoros pivoted to his right, glove loose on his right hand, and "run and run and run" as he would later say in his accented English, across the outfield and toward the suddenly distant corner.

On the field, torsos turned, heads snapped, and eyes focused on the sprinting outfielder. Home plate umpire Jim Honochick stepped aside from the now-standing Campanella to watch the flight of the ball and position himself to call the play at home everyone expected. Left field umpire John Flaherty moved toward the corner to make a fair/foul call, if needed. Podres jogged off the mound to back up third, head down in frustration of having been beaten on a good pitch. Hodges and Gilliam moved to cover their respective bases, their eyes trained on the outfield.

Martin stopped halfway between second and third, then turned his back to the plate to watch the ball drop in. Seeing the ball sailing to a deliciously vacant part of the field, McDougald flew around second toward third, hoping to score on what he was sure would be a game-tying double.

Reese kept an eye on McDougald, who was now jogging toward Martin, standing between the bases watching to make sure the ball dropped in. Hoping for a play at the plate, Reese moved onto the grass in short left near the line to await the cutoff throw from Amoros, who was still racing toward the fence.

Amoros, unaware of all the movement behind, around, and above him, had one eye on the ball, the other on the fast-approaching left field stands, a short step beyond the thick chalk foul line. Waiting until the last possible second after stepping onto the wide warning track, he planted on his right heel to avoid a collision with the fence. Coming to a jarring and momentary stop inches from the line, just in front of the 301 sign on the concrete leftfield wall, he stuck out his gloved right hand. Camera shutters clicked as the ball suddenly appeared in his dark leather mitt.

Amoros' stutter-step forward momentum brought him to the base of the left field fence in foul territory and, momentarily, face-to-face with stunned, white-shirted spectators in the stands. He held the snow-coned ball aloft like a trophy to make sure it didn't drop out of his mitt, and used his free left hand to brace himself against the waist-high fence top to regain his balance.

The Catch.

Back in the infield, Martin, unbelieving for a second, had time to dart back to second. But he had to wait for the incredulous McDougald, standing almost next to him in the base line, to whirl about-face and retag second on his frantic sprint back to first.

Naturally facing the infield after the catch, Amoros rifled a rope to the screaming Reese. Reese took the head-high throw in short left field near the line and, in one fluid motion, fired a long, letter-high strike across the diamond to an outstretched Hodges at first. Hodges snagged the throw just ahead of the sliding McDougald, finally finishing his backward race around the bases, to complete the double play.

"Well, my father cheered and yelled and called me back in," Camp reported, "and it was obviously before the day of instant replay, so I missed it. I was still a little leery, but I don't remember leaving the room again."

The Dodger enthusiasm was renewed, the Yankees deflated. With two down, Bauer grounded weakly to Reese to officially end the inning.

Hodges (#14) completes the sixth-inning rally-killing play as he catches the relay from Reese to double up McDougald after Amoros's catch.

Podres, despite being tired, was charged by the catch. To start the seventh, Skowron and Cerv both hit slow rollers to short that Reese was forced to charge and make off-balance throws on in order to get the outs. Howard singled with two out, but the crippled Mantle, pinch-hitting for Grim, undercut a towering popup behind third that Reese caught.

One minor threat ended, but another materialized in the eighth.

Rizzuto opened the inning with a line single to left-center. Martin attempted to hit a ball to the opposite field, but his soft liner to right was caught at the knees by a charging Furillo. McDougald smashed a ball down third that took a wicked hop off a backtracking Hoak's left shoulder into left field for a single.

Runners on first and second, again, and Berra up, again. Fans all over the city and in the stands sat up, Brooklynites nervous, Yankee fans expectant.

On a 3-1 count, Berra finally pulled a pitch, a fly to short right to Furillo for the second out. Fans slumped back in their seats, Brooklynites relieved, Yankee fans sensing the inevitable.

Bauer took a ball high and tight, then a called strike, fouled a pitch back to the screen, then took ball two. With the more than 62,000 fans screaming, Podres, now throwing nothing but heat, reached back and fired a high hard exclamation point. As he fell off the mound from the force of the pitch, Bauer swung and missed.

Ironically, the ninth was Podres' easiest inning of the game. Skowron hit a sharp one-hopper back to him, which Podres fielded with more luck than skill. The ball ripped the webbing and stuck between the fingers of the glove. Podres had trouble disentangling the ball, and decided to complete the play unassisted. But as he jogged toward first, he finally dislodged the ball and lobbed it to Hodges to nip the lumbering Moose.

One out.

Cerv hit a pop fly that Amoros easily gathered in in left.

Two out.

Howard strode to the plate, the Yankees' last hope.

"Well, it wasn't bedlam or anything like that," DeClemente noted from his vantage point in Section 11. "It was kind of quiet, except for a few of us yelling and jumping up and down. I'll tell you one thing: I don't like peanuts. I hate peanuts. And I was so nervous in that ninth inning that the peanut vendor came by and I said 'Give me two bags.' He threw two bags up to me, and I handed one to my brother-in-law. And I kept stuffing them in my mouth and spitting them out. I didn't know what to do with myself, because here it was, finally it looked like we were going to get it."

There was a more sober atmosphere in Kansas City. Bob Wedgeworth was home from college and was watching the game with his family. When former Kansas City Monarch star and only Yankee black player Elston Howard came to the plate, Wedgeworth experienced mixed feelings.

"Because Howard was known in the community nobody wanted to see him fail," Wedgeworth explains. "But they didn't want him to defeat the Dodgers. We didn't want him to fail, but we didn't want him to do anything extraordinary either."

Podres wasn't thinking about anything. He was operating on pure adrenaline and simply throwing as hard as he could. Howard took a called strike. Then a ball. A swing, a miss, a cheer — strike two. Ball, high. Two balls and two strikes.

Howard then proceeded to foul off fastball after fastball. After five pitches and five agonizing foul balls, Podres had had enough. Campy called for another heater, but Podres shook him off. The tired but stubborn lefty wanted to throw one last changeup.

"It was the only pitch I shook Campanella off the whole game," Podres said later. "I could see Howard swing where he was starting to get on my fastball and I shook Campanella off to get the change."

Campy relented. Howard, fooled by the floater, slapped a grounder to short, appropriately to the longest-suffering Dodger of them all, Reese.

After what seemed like hours to the proud Dodger captain, Reese surrounded the bouncer and threw a low, wide relay across the diamond to first. Hodges leaned and reached far to his left, his spiked toe nailed to the first base bag. He'd say later he'd have stretched across the Bronx to make the catch.

The myth of Yankee invincibility was broken. Next year was here.

THE CELEBRATION

When Hodges reached out for Reese's throw from shortstop, New York — and especially Brooklyn — exploded. Someone grabbed Podres' leg, someone else grabbed his arm, Campanella grabbed him around the waist, Hoak jumped on all of them. Dodgers poured from the field, dugout, and bullpen, fans streamed out of the stands — all headed for a pile-on on Podres.

Down on Wall Street, little trading was done in the usual frenzied closing minutes of the stock exchange session. On lower Broadway, a puzzled foreigner couldn't get a satisfactory explanation for all the confetti and ticker tape raining down on him from the skyscrapers lining the Canyon of Heroes. "Dodgers?" he was heard to mutter after receiving a mangled explanation. "Yankees? What are those?"

From precisely 3:44 pm, a minute after the final out, to 4:01 pm, it was practically impossible to get a dial tone on phones along the east side of Manhattan. Fans lucky enough to connect could not raise the outer boroughs. The Murray Hill, Lexington, Oregon, Plaza, Templeton, and Eldorado exchanges were overloaded by calls from diehards collecting on bets, arranging celebration dinners, and exchanging expressions of communal joy. According

to the phone company, it handled the largest volume of calls since VJ Day 10 years before.

In Witherbee, New York, Mrs. Podres was in tears and couldn't speak. Johnny's 19-year-old girlfriend, Naomi Baker, glowed. "He's wonderful, just wonderful! I sure wish I'd been there to see it. I was there for all the other games. Isn't that terrible, to miss seeing Johnny like that?"

On E. 48th Street in Canarsie, people came pouring out of their houses. Audrey Tassone, crying tears of joy, walked across the street and collected her $2 bet from Jack Harkavy. "We were so excited, we couldn't eat," says Audrey. "People were calling one another. 'Well, did you see the game?' 'Of course I saw the game!' We saw some of the key replays on television, exalting each good move they made."

The rest of Brooklyn was in bedlam. Flatbush Avenue exploded in a cacophony of car horns. Kings Highway, Atlantic Avenue, Ocean Parkway, 86th Street, and Fourth Avenue were all sites for impromptu parades. There were traffic jams at two sections of Fulton Street; a seven-block gridlock centered at Nostrand Avenue took 90 minutes to clear, and a six-block stopper at Flatbush Avenue didn't untangle for an hour. A truck carrying decaying fruits, vegetables, and horn-blowing urchins careened through Flatbush. At the corner of DeKalb and Flatbush, the motley-crewed vehicle sped past a man who observed that the kids "were the spirit of all the Series games the Dodgers lost."

Smiling cops ignored the bumper-car-like driving on the streets and

3:43 pm, October 4, 1955, The Bronx, NY. Podres is apoplectic as Campy chases him down after Howard grounded out — Reese to Hodges — to make the Brooklyn Dodgers World Champions.

stowed their traffic ticket books for the afternoon. When asked what could be done about the traffic mess, one patrolman said, "Nothing. Besides, I'm a Dodger fan myself."

Pool rooms and bars filled with revelers releasing the pent-up frustrations of almost a half century of World Series failure. In the Concord Inn at 308 Fulton Street, the boss, Gus Caminiti, yelled to his bartender, Bill Smith, at precisely 3:45:30: "Drinks! Drinks for every bum in the house! Next year we win it in four!"

At the Edison Bar at 242 Flatbush Avenue, the cash register was the only thing not making noise. "This is something Brooklyn will remember for years," said glassy-eyed owner John Mangol, but no one knew if he was referring to the Dodgers or the free drinks.

The Dodger Bar at Flatbush Avenue Extension and DeKalb Avenue went berserk as the game ended. Stools flew in the air, women danced on the bar. Ann Margot of 2822 W. 27th Street, quietly fainted at her table. A panhandler strode up to the bar, put a $1 bill on the counter and said: "Set me up! I've been a Dodger fan for 20 years. I'm knocking off work for the day."

Andy Mangano, restaurant owner at 334 Court Street, put a keg of free beer and a jukebox outside on the sidewalk, which prompted dancing in the street.

Joseph Saden, owner of Joe's Delicatessen at 324 Utica Avenue, went absolutely stark raving and certifiably mad by Brooklyn standards: he opened a sidewalk stand and actually gave away hot dogs.

Dodgers and Dodger fans charge Podres. . .

. . . but his ecstatic teammates reach him first.

David Karp, owner of a candy store at 50 Smith Street, handed out 50 cigars. "It's like having a baby," he beamed.

In front of a Livingston Street bootblack stand, an elderly man with a long white beard leaned on his cane and muttered, "I never thought I'd live so long."

Jack White of 1954 36th Street noted that "I've gone back to Ireland and I've seen the Dodgers win. Now I'm ready to die. May the Lord have mercy on me."

Pillows mushed into vaguely human form and crudely labeled "Yankees" were hung in effigy from lampposts. Firecrackers flamed and exploded, pots and pans were clanked on brownstone stoops and out of upper-story windows. Hundreds crammed into the creaking Hotel Bossert, where the official victory celebration was scheduled.

At the Brooklyn office of Silver Shield, Larry King and his workmates had been listening to the game over the radio. "I couldn't work the rest of the day. I went out in the street in the heart of downtown Brooklyn and the mayhem was — I mean, horns were blowing ... I couldn't wait to get home. On the subway train everyone was smiling and we didn't know what to do with ourselves. Finally I got to the neighborhood and I just went crazy. The first person I looked for was Herbie, who was the Yankee fan, just to taunt him, and taunt him. He felt terrible and said Mantle had been hurt; he always had an excuse. I was just jumping up and down, I was beside myself. The day became a blur."

The victory celebration
continues on the field. That's
a bare-headed Podres trying
to squeeze through the crowd
on the far left.

In Marine Park, Stan Keizerstein, who considered himself more sane than his Brooklyn compatriots, sat stunned and reflective. "I was more shocked than anything else. I was plain shocked. I couldn't believe that we had actually won, after so many years of frustration. And the Yankees — to beat the Yankees, that was like reaching the moon. It was a feeling of — the thrill of victory as they say. The final, final step. The top of the mountain. I think I celebrated with a can of beer or something like that, nothing serious, but there was a hell of a lot of noise on the streets and the roars that went up all around Brooklyn. My neighborhood was like every other one and the excitement was tremendous and it stayed with us for a long time."

In New Rochelle, Kaminer got out of old Hadassah K. Holmes' class feeling buoyant. He and Earl Ehrenstein sprinted the eight blocks to his buddy's house, then to the local W.T. Grant department store for several rounds of strawberry sundaes. "It was the 11-year old equivalent of getting drunk," Kaminer noted. "I could not control myself."

In Morristown, Camp jumped on his bicycle and prepared to make like Paul Revere. "I had this American flag set, you know, on little sticks that would sit in a holder, it was on my handlebars. I remember taking the middle flag off the middle one and putting a Dodger pennant in there and driving around, riding around the neighborhood yelling. I seemed to be alone. It seemed like there were Yankee fans all around me. It seemed like I was the only (Dodger fan). I celebrated alone. I reveled in it. I reveled in victory."

In the Catskills, Genalo had a little fun after putting up with Yankee taunts for the previous two-and-a-half hours. "I left the bar very happily yelling a few things to the people up there. And they were all rather glum. It was a very glum bar."

The celebrating wasn't limited to the United States. All over Latin America, the joy was no less heartfelt for the team that had opened major league clubhouse doors for blacks and Latinos. Cubans, especially residents of the old Spanish settlement of Matanzas, Amoros' birthplace, had listened to the game on their radios, the transmission courtesy of a plane flying between the island nation and Miami. In St. Thomas, capital of the Virgin Islands, 5,000 people, carrying signs such as "At Last — Brooklyn Wins" and "Snider — Duke of Bedford Avenue," paraded for four hours. The Garcia family of Ciudad Trujillo in the Dominican Republic, where the Dodgers had trained in 1948, named their newborn son "Podres."

Back in the Bronx, Sharff and his fellow "idiots" stormed out of the Stadium intent on exacting tribute from the local inhabitants. They paraded up and down the Grand Concourse from 161st Street to 186th Street and back, marching and chanting, "We won! We beat you!"

"The initial reaction was pure emotion," Sharff recalled. "First tears and then a defiant 'Up yours, The Bronx because we finally got you.' " Eventually, Sharff's group made their way back down to Yankee Stadium to try and catch

**Joyous teens cruise Brooklyn
streets celebrating.**

a glimpse of their heroes.

Pat DeClemente stuck around the Stadium for the same reason, but it was the Yankees who emerged, not the Dodgers. And the disappointed local partisans acted how they imagined Brooklyn bumpkins behaved. "We saw McDougald come out...outside, near the parking lot. And people were taunting him. Yankee fans were taunting him. And I kind of felt sorry for the guy. And then we saw Rizzuto come out, and you know, he was pretty glum. And a couple other guys who I don't remember, but I was just curious about it. Guys were throwing questions at him, mostly taunting him, saying not very nice things to him...The Yankee fans, you know, they didn't expect to lose. You know, whereas we, Dodger fans...something always happened."

Within the innards of the stadium, anyone who wandered inside the Dodger clubhouse was instantly bathed with champagne and beer. Podres was slumped against his locker, his head resting on a towel pillow. Reporters surrounded him, yelled out disjointed questions and got bold answers.

"My fastball really had it."

"Mantle? I wasn't worried about him. I keep my fastball up on him, and he can't hit it."

"I was never really worried about anybody."

"I can beat these guys seven days a week."

Suddenly he realized what he was saying and politely asked the writers to ignore his bravado. "It sounds too much like I'm popping off."

He introduced the older gentleman standing near him. "That's my uncle. He tells me my father is outside in the car. He won't come in. He's crying." Podres giggled nervously. "My father is crying," he repeated with incredulity. But Johnny admitted he couldn't. "It's all right, Johnny," his uncle consoled him. "Cry. I did."

Clem Labine cried. Furillo started yelling, "To hell with Billy Cox! And DiMaggio! And Dressen!" All three had been quoted saying the Yankees would win because the Dodgers always folded. "Print it in big letters," Furillo shouted. "Tell Billy Cox we didn't choke up. Tell him we won it — without him!"

Amoros, alternately sucking on a huge Cuban cigar and a can of beer, was explaining his catch in broken English. "I kept my eyes on the ball — never looked anywhere else. It stayed up just long enough to fall into my glove like this." He pantomimed the catch. "I never hit fence, but I was only this far from it." He spread his cigar and beer can about 20 inches apart.

At that moment, O'Malley came up behind him and grabbed the happy outfielder by the shoulders. "Where's that $100 you owe me?" referring to the fine Amoros was assessed by Bavasi for reporting late to spring training. No one was quite sure if O'Malley was kidding.

Outside the stadium, Robinson addressed a crowd of wildly cheering fans. "This is the real Brooklyn," Robinson shouted. "The whole team knows it was the fans that made it for us. It was their support that put the zing into us."

Cuban Amoros basks in the glow of a home-grown stogie.

**Podres gets a Schaefer shower
from his teammates in the
lockerroom.**

Podres was struck by the number of cops outside, playing Moses by clearing a path for the players to the team bus. "I was in the middle of all those cops and I said, 'Look at this, this is something else.' I remember getting on the bus and everyone giving me a hand, the players and the wives that were on the bus. It was touching, real touching. It was some day, some day in Brooklyn Dodger history. It was some day over in Brooklyn that night."

The differences between the reserve of the rest of the city and the emotional, wild abandon of Brooklyn were illustrated in stark terms for Dodger announcer Vin Scully, driving from the Bronx to Brooklyn later that evening for the official victory celebration.

"When the Yankees won a World Series, the Bronx didn't go bananas, and when the Giants won in their great heyday, I don't think Manhattan danced in the streets. But when Brooklyn won the World Series, the borough went wild. It was like us against the world.

"After the last game in Yankee Stadium, we were driving from Yankee Stadium back toward Brooklyn. And you could almost see as the lights were

A rare public expression of pure joy from O'Malley (middle), witnessed by a bemused Alston (left) and a weary but happy Reese (right).

coming on in Manhattan that football was around the corner and everything was quiet, the fall had moved in very, very quietly.

"But suddenly when we went through the Brooklyn Battery Tunnel and came out the other side it was a whole new world. The people were just going wild. Dancing in the streets, it was like VJ Day. I mean, the joy in the streets, the block parties, the streets roped off. We had to park, as I remember it, about two blocks from the hotel and we had to walk. The police had set up saw horses and everything else. There were hundreds and hundreds of people on the sidewalks and they were cheering and screaming as you walked down the street toward the hotel. It was an incredible night."

At the Bossert, 2,000 people crowded behind the police barricades in front of the old hotel. Snider, Robinson, Campy, Furillo, Zimmer, Loes, Hoak, and Amoros all made it past the crowds and into the Gold Room for the victory party.

Podres was late because of an appearance on Steve Allen's TV program, "The Tonight Show." Podres and Hodges, also tardy, had just about reached

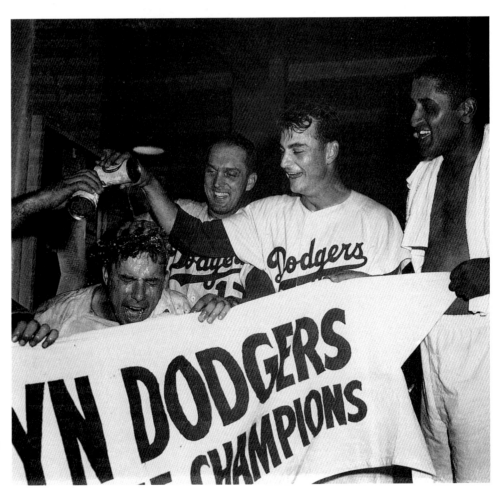

Captain Reese holds up the long overdue championship banner and gets a soaking from Erskine, Bessent, and Newcombe.

Outside the Hotel Bossert,
throngs wait for their heros
to arrive for the official celebration, October 4, 1955.

The celebration inside the Hotel Bossert. That's Podres tripping the light fantastic in the middle of the dance floor.

the hotel door when a fan yelled, "Come here! We want to shake hands!" Both players dashed across the street, pushed aside the barricades, and lost themselves in the hand-pumping, back-thumping crowd for 15 minutes before working their way back to the hotel.

Brooklyn borough president John Cashmore held court for reporters. With the polished enthusiasm of a politician, he promised an immediate survey of a possible site for a new stadium for the Dodgers at Atlantic and Flatbush avenues. With the sun setting behind him, he proclaimed that the Dodgers "must never leave Brooklyn!"

1955 WORLD SERIES STATISTICS

DODGERS

PLAYER/POS	AVG	G	AB	R	H	2B	3B	HR	RBI	BB	SO	SB
Sandy Amoros, of	.333	5	12	3	4	0	0	1	3	4	4	0
Don Bessent, p	.000	3	1	0	0	0	0	0	0	0	1	0
Roy Campanella, c	.259	7	27	4	7	3	0	2	4	3	3	0
Roger Craig, p	.000	1	0	0	0	0	0	0	0	1	0	0
Carl Erskine, p	.000	1	1	0	0	0	0	0	0	0	0	0
Carl Furillo, of	.296	7	27	4	8	1	0	1	3	3	5	0
Jim Gilliam, 2b-5,of-4	.292	7	24	2	7	1	0	0	3	8	1	1
Don Hoak, 3b-1	.333	3	3	0	1	0	0	0	0	2	0	0
Gil Hodges, 1b	.292	7	24	2	7	0	0	1	5	3	2	0
Frank Kellert, ph	.333	3	3	0	1	0	0	0	0	0	0	0
Clem Labine, p	.000	4	4	0	0	0	0	0	0	0	3	0
Billy Loes, p	.000	1	1	0	0	0	0	0	0	0	0	0
Russ Meyer, p	.000	1	2	0	0	0	0	0	0	0	1	0
Don Newcombe, p	.000	1	3	0	0	0	0	0	0	0	0	0
Johnny Podres, p	.143	2	7	1	1	0	0	0	0	0	1	0
Pee Wee Reese, ss	.296	7	27	5	8	1	0	0	2	3	5	0
Jackie Robinson, 3b	.182	6	22	5	4	1	1	0	1	2	1	1
Ed Roebuck, p	.000	1	0	0	0	0	0	0	0	0	0	0
George Shuba, ph	.000	1	1	0	0	0	0	0	0	0	0	0
Duke Snider, of	.320	7	25	5	8	1	0	4	7	2	6	0
Karl Spooner, p	.000	2	0	0	0	0	0	0	0	0	0	0
Don Zimmer, 2b	.222	4	9	0	2	0	0	0	2	2	5	0
TEAM TOTAL	.260	7	223	31	58	8	1	9	30	33	38	2

PITCHERS	W	L	ERA	G	GS	CG	SV	IP	H	ER	BB	SO
Don Bessent	0	0	0.00	3	0	0	0	3.1	3	0	1	1
Roger Craig	1	0	3.00	1	1	0	0	6.0	4	2	5	4
Carl Erskine	0	0	9.00	1	1	0	0	3.0	3	3	2	3
Clem Labine	1	0	2.89	4	0	0	1	9.1	6	3	2	2
Billy Loes	0	1	9.82	1	1	0	0	3.2	7	4	1	5
Russ Meyer	0	0	0.00	1	0	0	0	5.2	4	0	2	4
Don Newcombe	0	1	9.53	1	1	0	0	5.2	8	6	2	4
Johnny Podres	2	0	1.00	2	2	2	0	18.0	15	2	4	10
Ed Roebuck	0	0	0.00	1	0	0	0	2.0	1	0	0	0
Karl Spooner	0	1	13.50	2	1	0	0	3.1	4	5	3	6
TEAM TOTAL	4	3	3.75		7	2	1	60.0	55	25	22	39

YANKEES

PLAYER/POS	AVG	G	AB	R	H	2B	3B	HR	RBI	BB	SO	SB
Hank Bauer, of-5	.429	6	14	1	6	0	0	0	1	0	1	0
Yogi Berra, c	.417	7	24	5	10	1	0	1	2	3	1	0
Tommy Byrne, p-2	.167	3	6	0	1	0	0	0	2	0	2	0
Andy Carey, ph	.500	2	2	0	1	0	1	0	1	0	0	0
Tom Carroll, pr	.000	2	0	0	0	0	0	0	0	0	0	0
Bob Cerv, of-4	.125	5	16	1	2	0	0	1	1	0	4	0
Gerry Coleman, ss	.000	3	3	0	0	0	0	0	0	0	1	0
Rip Coleman, p	.000	1	0	0	0	0	0	0	0	0	0	0
Joe Collins, 1b-5,of-1	.167	5	12	6	2	0	0	2	3	6	4	1
Whitey Ford, p	.000	2	6	1	0	0	0	0	0	1	1	0
Bob Grim, p	.000	3	2	0	0	0	0	0	0	0	0	0
Elston Howard, of	.192	7	26	3	5	0	0	1	3	1	8	0
Johnny Kucks, p	.000	2	0	0	0	0	0	0	0	0	0	0
Don Larsen, p	.000	1	2	0	0	0	0	0	0	0	0	0
Mickey Mantle, of-2	.200	3	10	1	2	0	0	1	1	0	2	0
Billy Martin, 2b	.320	7	25	2	8	1	1	0	4	1	5	0
Gil Mc Dougald, 3b	.259	7	27	2	7	0	0	1	1	2	6	0
Tom Morgan, p	.000	2	0	0	0	0	0	0	0	0	0	0
Irv Noren, of	.063	5	16	0	1	0	0	0	1	1	1	0
Phil Rizzuto, ss	.267	7	15	2	4	0	0	0	1	5	1	2
Eddie Robinson, 1b-1	.667	4	3	0	2	0	0	0	1	2	1	0
Bill Skowron, 1b-3	.333	5	12	2	4	2	0	1	3	0	1	0
Tom Sturdivant, p	.000	2	0	0	0	0	0	0	0	0	0	0
Bob Turley, p	.000	3	1	0	0	0	0	0	0	0	0	0
TEAM TOTAL	.248	7	222	26	55	4	2	8	25	22	39	3

PITCHERS	W	L	ERA	G	GS	CG	SV	IP	H	ER	BB	SO
Tommy Byrne	1	1	1.88	2	2	1	0	14.1	8	3	8	8
Rip Coleman	0	0	9.00	1	0	0	0	1.0	5	1	0	1
Whitey Ford	2	0	2.12	2	2	1	0	17.0	13	4	8	10
Bob Grim	0	1	4.15	3	1	0	1	8.2	8	4	5	8
Johnny Kucks	0	0	6.00	2	0	0	0	3.0	4	2	1	1
Don Larsen	0	1	11.25	1	1	0	0	4.0	5	5	2	2
Tom Morgan	0	0	4.91	2	0	0	0	3.2	3	2	3	1
Tom Sturdivant	0	0	6.00	2	0	0	0	3.0	5	2	2	0
Bob Turley	0	1	8.44	3	1	0	0	5.1	7	5	4	7
TEAM TOTAL	3	4	4.20		7	2	1	60.0	58	28	33	38

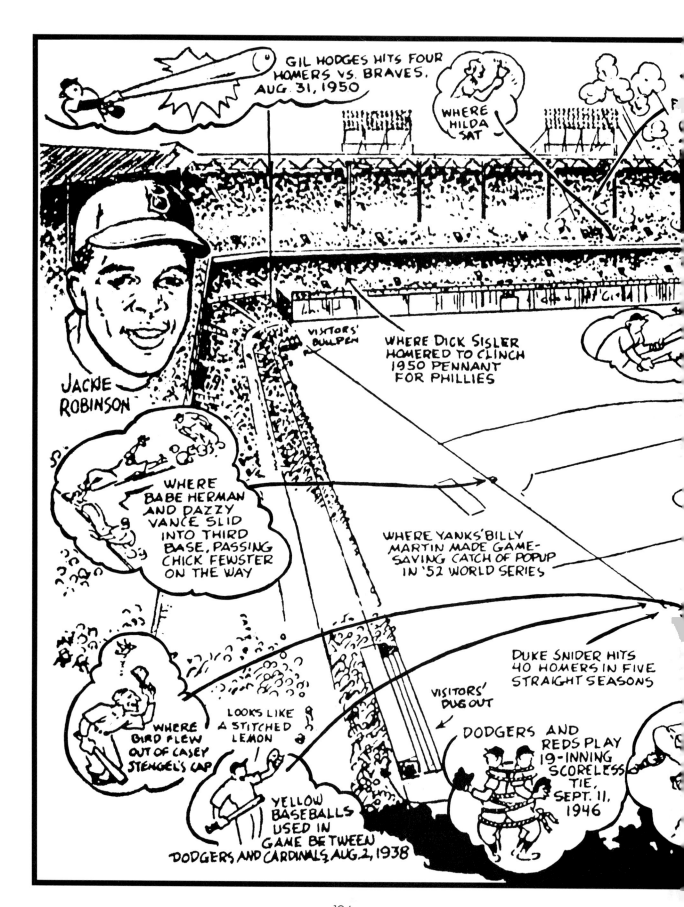

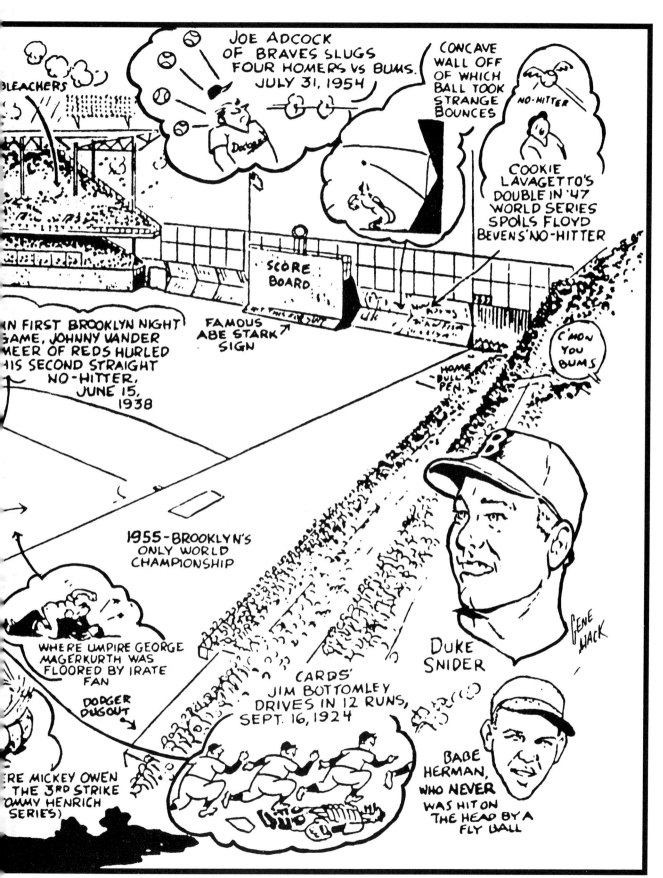

Gene Mack's cartoon of Ebbets Field. (updated)

PHOTOGRAPHS AND ILLUSTRATIONS